Charles University in Prague
Karolinum Press

THE PRAGUE

OF CHARLES IV

Jan Royt

Translated by Derek and Marzia Paton

Karolinum Press

Originally published in Czech under the title *Praha Karla IV*, Prague: Karolinum 2016
KAROLINUM PRESS, Ovocný trh 3–5, 116 36 Prague 1, Czech Republic
Karolinum Press is a publishing department of Charles University in Prague
www.karolinum.cz

Edited by Milada Motlová (Czech) and Martin Janeček (English)
Cover and graphic design by Zdeněk Ziegler
Maps by Jaroslav Synek
Typeset by DTP Karolinum
Printed in the Czech Republic by Tiskárny Havlíčkův Brod, a. s.
First English edition
ISBN 978-80-246-3132-5

The manuscript was reviewed by Vladimír Hrubý, PhDr (Institute of History, University of Pardubice)
and Professor Petr Sommer, PhDr (director of the Centre for Medieval Studies, Prague)

The "Prague" series is edited by Milada Motlová

This book was kindly supported by the ministry of Culture of the Czech Republic.

MINISTRY OF CULTURE
CZECH REPUBLIC

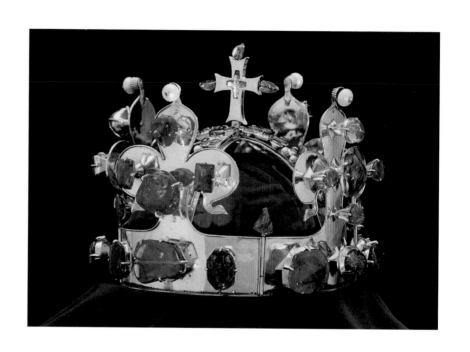

CONTENTS

The Prague of Charles IV   /11

The Prague of Charles IV: A guide to the city   /61

Who was Charles IV?   /180
Forebears and descendants of Charles IV   /182
Eminent persons of Charles IV's day and later   /184
A map of Prague   /188
A map of Prague castle   /190
A floor plan of St Vitus' cathedral   /191
The Caroline cross of Prague   /192

Acknowledgements   /194
List of illustrations   /195
About the author   /199

THE PRAGUE OF CHARLES IV

The year was 1333, the month October, when the heir to the Bohemian crown, the firstborn son of John of Luxembourg and Elizabeth of Bohemia (Eliška Přemyslovna, in Czech), returned to Prague; he was seventeen years old. Though baptized Wenceslas (Václav), during his seven years at the court of the king of France – to which he was related through the Luxembourgs – he took the name Charles at his Confirmation, after Charles IV, King of France, called the Fair. One of the reasons why his father had isolated the young Charles from his mother and then sent him to France to be brought up, from 1323 to 1330, was that relations between King John and his wife were strained because of their different views about policy in the kingdom of Bohemia, but it was also a custom of the Luxembourgs to ensure their scions a French upbringing. At the French court the young prince was entrusted to the care of private tutors and instructors, including Pierre Roger, the future Pope Clement VI. In Paris Charles learnt French and Latin, the rudiments of the arts, philosophy, and theology, and it is assumed that he attended lectures at the University of Paris. He was also well versed in the lively medieval French academy and culture. The marriage of Charles, a Bohemian prince, and Blanche of Valois, a French princess, in 1323, while they were still children, reinforced the bond between the French and the Bohemian throne.

In 1330 John of Luxembourg charged his adolescent son with governing and defending with the sword his possessions in Italy, particularly the cities of Lombardy and Tuscany. After the Battle of San Felice, fought on the Feast of St Catherine, 1332, the sixteen-year-old Charles was dubbed a knight. And it was written about him that he 'fought well as a knight in battle'. His first military victories in Italy boosted the self-confidence of the young prince to the extent that near Lucca he established a fortress and settlement bearing his name: Montecarlo. Charles will have certainly encountered new fashions in art in Italy, which is attested to, for example, by his taste for the paintings of Tomaso da Modena. In 1333 the leading nobles of Bohemia set off for Italy in order to beseech the crown prince to return to Bohemia, which was suffering during the long absence of the king. Charles responded to their request, and in August 1333, after his defeat in battle near Ferrara he headed for the frontiers of Bohemia instead of Lucca as planned. His first steps led to the Cistercian abbey of Zbraslav, just south of Prague, to the tomb of his mother, Elizabeth. It is possible that it was on this occasion that he donated to the abbey the panel painting called the *Madonna of Zbraslav*, by the Master of the Vyšebrod Altar. Apart from this visit to the burial places of his mother and the last Přemyslids, his Přemyslid ancestry is also reflected in the Bohemian coronation liturgy which he had a large part in drawing up. In it he stipulated that on the eve of the coronation the future monarch must visit Vyšehrad at Prague, and put on the bast shoes and take the satchel of the founder of the dynasty, Přemysl the Ploughman.

The Bohemian Crown

The Bohemian Crown, called the Crown of St Wenceslas, is the foremost symbol of the Bohemian Lands. Charles IV, who had ordered it made in 1344–45 and had then been crowned with it, decreed that the Bohemian Crown belonged to Wenceslas, the ever-lasting heir to the Lands of Bohemia; the monarch merely was entrusted with the crown, and for that he had to pay a large sum of money to St Vitus' Chapter, which 'represented' the saint. The Bohemian Crown is a reliquary crown: a thorn of Christ's Crown of Thorns was placed into its cross of rock crystal. The crown could be worn only by the rightful ruler.

This splendid piece of jewellery is made of pure gold, decorated with 91 gemstones (sapphires, spinels, emeralds, and rubies) and 20 pearls. To make the crown, a precious girdle of Queen Blanche of Valois was used. Beginning in 1358, the crown rested on the reliquary bust of St Wenceslas, which was placed on his tomb in the Wenceslas Chapel at St Vitus' Cathedral. It was moved to the Crown Chamber, located above the Wenceslas Chapel, probably during the Hussite Wars (1419–c.1434).

The door leading to the Crown Chamber directly from the Wenceslas Chapel has seven locks. The tradition of seven keepers of the keys began in the late eighteenth century, when the Office of the Keepers of the Bohemian Crown Jewels was established. In the course of the nineteenth and twentieth centuries, the structure of the keepers of the keys changed as regimes changed. At present the keys are kept by the seven highest representatives of the State, the Church, and the City, that is, the President of the Republic, the Prime Minister, and the Archbishop of Prague, the Speaker of the Senate of the Parliament of the Czech Republic, the Speaker of the Chamber of Deputies of the Parliament of the Czech Republic, the Provost of the Metropolitan Chapter of St Vitus', and the Mayor of Prague, Capital of the Czech Republic.

A Coronation

For his coronation as King of Bohemia, which took place in the Basilica of St Vitus' on 2 September 1347, Charles IV also created a new order of service. To do so, he drew on the order of service for the coronation not only of the Bohemian ruling house of Přemyslid, but also of the King of the Romans and the King of France. Charles's coronation began at Vyšehrad on the evening of 1 September 1347. In keeping with the new order of service he took possession of the Přemyslid relics – the bast shoes and the satchel of Přemysl the Ploughman, the mythical founder of the dynasty. Later that evening, Charles was ritually put to bed and then ritually awakened the next morning. Then, in the procession that carried the royal regalia, the cross and sword of St Wenceslas, Charles was led to the basilica, where the actual coronation took place. Archbishop Ernest of Pardubice first anointed Charles with the chrism, then dressed him in the ceremonial robes, dubbed him with the sword, and then placed the Crown of St Wenceslas on his head.

(15)

When he returned to Bohemia the young Charles at first spoke Italian, Latin, German, and French far better than his mother tongue. Nevertheless, he soon mastered Czech. A year later, in 1334, his wife, Blanche, also arrived in Prague with her retinue. She was the daughter of Charles I, Count of Valois, and Mahaut of Châtillon, his third wife. Her brother was Philip VI, the future king of France. Charles's favourite wife, Blanche (baptized Marguerite) quickly learnt Czech and German, but mostly avoided society. She remained in the Bohemian Lands even when Charles was abroad. On 25 May 1335, their first child, Margaret, was born. Margaret was later married to Louis I, King of Hungary (she died in 1349). Their second daughter, born in 1342, was called Catherine. She married Rudolph IV, Duke of Austria (a Habsburg, and self-proclaimed archduke). After his death, she married Otto V, Duke of Bavaria.

In early 1334, King John appointed his son Margrave of Moravia. A year later, Charles, together with his father, met with the new king of Poland, Casimir III, in Trenčín (Upper Hungary, today's Slovakia). Here, John waived his claim to the Polish throne and in return Casimir acknowledged John's rule in Silesia and the Duchy of Głogów. In 1337, the two Luxembourgs set out together on a crusade against the pagan Lithuanians. In that same year John (now blind in one eye) left for France to help Philip VI against the English (at the start of what became known as the Hundred Years' War). Charles, as Margrave of Moravia, reinforced the power of the throne in Moravia when he succeeded in bringing the recalcitrant Moravian nobles into line. He also negotiated with the Angevine Charles Robert of Hungary. At the Bohemian Diet, on 11 June 1341, the now completely blind John conferred on Charles the title *rex iunior* (junior king).

After coming to Prague, Charles found the seat of the kings of Bohemia at Prague Castle – and other things – in a dismal state. As he writes in his autobiography, *Vita Caroli*: 'We discovered this kingdom so devastated that we were unable to find any castle or crown property that was not mortgaged. Consequently, we had nowhere to stay except in the burgher manner in a burgher's house.'

The royal palace had been empty since 1303, and Charles IV decided to rebuild it on French models. Its centre was a great hall decorated with panel paintings portraying Charles's forebears on the imperial throne. (Later, under Jagiellon rule, in the fifteenth and the sixteenth century, it would be rebuilt as Wladislaus Hall.)

During his sojourns in France and Italy, Charles IV came to know the art and architecture of the two countries. France already had grand cathedrals, and Paris could boast three royal palaces and many fine noble houses. In Italy, he could see not only churches decorated with mosaics, but also works by Giotto, members of the Pisano family, and Martini. In the Sainte-Chapelle, Paris, Charles found inspiration for the Chapel of All Saints at his own court, which took the place of a twelfth-century chapel. Here, in 1341, Charles founded a chapter whose members were university masters. In 1366, it was incorporated into the Caroline College of Prague University. The elegant new building, with three bays of vaulting, was erected from 1370 to 1387 on plans by Peter Parler. This is skeletal architecture: the walls of the church were pierced by great windows filled with Flamboyant tracery. The interiors were encrusted with gemstones. (The original appearance of the chapel was wiped away by the great fire of 1541.) Charles IV also saw to reinforcing the Castle defences, and he put gilded lead sheet on the roofs of the Black Tower and the White Tower at Prague Castle.

In 1341, after heated disputes with the Diet, King John officially proclaimed Charles the rightful heir to the throne. Among the first important political acts of the successor to the Bohemian throne was his role in raising the diocese of Prague to an archdiocese.

The Přemyslid rulers of Bohemia had already tried, but in vain, to free the Bohemian Lands from their bonds to the archdiocese of Mainz (the largest ecclesiastical province of Germany) and to establish their own archdiocese. The success of the Luxembourgs in this was undoubtedly thanks in part to Charles, who was already considerably involved in ruling the Bohemian Lands. The king of Bohemia and his son set out for Avignon to visit Pope Clement VI in the spring of 1344. Their talks led to, among other things, the raising of the diocese of Prague to an archdiocese by a papal bull issued on 30 April 1344. The creation of the archdiocese of Prague was of immense importance not only for Church life in the country, but also for Bohemian statehood: from that time onwards, the kings of Bohemia could be crowned by local archbishops. The founding of St Vitus' Cathedral, which was meant to be a place of coronation, pilgrimage, and commemoration, is also related to the establishment of the archdiocese. It was, however, also perceived as an expression of royal representation. The first foundation stones of the Cathedral of Sts Vitus, Wenceslas, and Adalbert, as it is officially known, were laid by the two Luxembourgs and the new Archbishop of Prague, Ernest of Pardubice, at a ceremony on 21 November 1344. Construction work on the cathedral did not begin on greenfield land; it was erected on a site where Duke Wenceslas had built a rotunda in c.930, which other Přemyslids later rebuilt into a Romanesque basilica of two choirs. John of Luxembourg promised tithes from the silver mines (those already in operation and those that would be opened in future) for the construction of the cathedral. He thus wanted to provide compensation for having stripped the tomb of St Adalbert of its silver statuary. In addition to income from the silver mines, the building was financed with collections announced by the archbishop and from pilgrimages and also contributions from courtiers, some of whom were donors of individual chapels.

To build St Vitus' Cathedral, Charles invited a French architect, Matthew of Arras. Matthew had found inspiration in the cathedrals of Rodez and Narbonne in the south of France, as is evident from the plan of the cathedral choir with the apse formed by five sides of a decagon, an ambulatory with the same number of sides, and choir chapels, each of whose apses is formed by five sides of an octagon. The characteristic features of Matthew's architecture are the robust arcades on the ground floor and the thick walls. Summoned from Avignon to Prague by Charles, Matthew was in charge of the construction work from 1344 until his death in 1352. Four years later, the 23-year-old Peter Parler took over as master of works. He came to Prague from Gmünd in Swabia, and worked in Bohemia for the next forty years. His forward-looking architectural style was then spread throughout Europe by his pupils. He unified the space of the choir by means of net vaulting. The Parler lodge also used dynamic elements such as the pendants (large bosses) in the old sacristy and the Flamboyant motifs in the tracery. Before 1385, Parler and his lodge succeeded in finishing the choir and much of the Great Tower (on the south side). In 1392, the foundations of the nave and aisles were laid, and, four years later, the tomb of St Adalbert was inserted into the centre of this space. Peter Parler was also

Matthew of Arras

When he came from Avignon to Prague, summoned by Charles IV, Matthew of Arras, the first master mason of St Vitus' Cathedral, had already built two cathedrals in the south of France, in Rodez and Narbonne. He was in charge of the building of St Vitus' from 1344 until the end of his life in 1352 (after which Peter Parler took over). As the first master mason of this cathedral, he was also given a place of honour in the gallery of eminent persons in the inner triforium.

a sculptor in stone and wood. When he died, in 1399, his sons continued his work in the cathedral.

At that time, one entered St Vitus' from the south gate, which faces the town. It is decorated with a magnificent mosaic, whose gold background, in the glow of the sun, created an aureole over the seat of the kings of Bohemia – which is why it came to be called the Golden Gate. It was from here that the newly crowned monarch or the monarch's funeral procession used to leave the cathedral, and it was also through this porch that crowds of pilgrims used to enter. The splendid mosaic on the Golden Gate was commissioned by the Emperor Charles IV in 1370–71, shortly after returning from his second coronation journey to Italy, this time to Rome to be crowned Emperor. The mosaic was designed by the Italian painter Niccolò (Nicoletto) Semitecolo, and work was begun by Venetian mosaicists, who then trained Bohemian artisans. The mosaic covers the whole wall above the three pointed arches of the south entrance.

Charles IV further declared his Přemyslid origins by having the bodies of the dukes and kings of Bohemia buried in the choir chapels, in tombs decorated with their effigies, each standing on a lion. In the Chapel of St John the Baptist are buried Břetislav II and Bořivoj II, and in the Imperial Chapel, Břetislav I and Spytihněv II; in the Chapel of the Relics (also known as the Saxon Chapel) are the tombs of Ottokar I and Ottokar II. An important place in the conception of the cathedral is held by the triforium, which is decorated with the busts of the imperial family, the archbishops of Prague, the clerks of works, and even the master masons from 1373 to 1375.

Peter Parler

At the age of twenty-three, the architect and sculptor in stone and wood from Gmünd, near Stuttgart, took over from the late French master mason at St Vitus' Cathedral, but he adapted Matthew's plans to suit his own style. Before 1385, Parler and his lodge succeeded in completing the choir and a considerable part of the Great Tower on the south side. After his death, Parler's sons continued working on the cathedral. The work of the Parler lodge at the cathedral includes the gallery of 21 stone busts in the triforium. His own bust is part of this group of portraits, carved from 1380 to 1382, of distinguished figures of Charles's court, mostly linked with the cathedral. Parler worked in Bohemia for forty years, and his forward-looking architectural style was then spread by his pupils throughout Europe.

An ideological focal point of the cathedral is the Wenceslas Chapel, where Duke Wenceslas (*c*.907–935 or 929), the 'born heir of the Bohemian Lands', is buried. The sanctity of the place is expressed by, among other things, the fact that the tomb of Wenceslas, since the translation of his mortal remains from Stará Boleslav to Prague shortly after his death, has always been here. The chapel was completed on the eve of the Feast of St Wenceslas, 1366. It was consecrated by the Archbishop of Prague, John Očko of Vlašim, on 30 November 1367. The Wenceslas Chapel is built on a square plan and covered with net vaulting. It has two portals. A door, later decorated with the initials of Władysław Jagiełło (Ladislas Jagiellon), has a knocker in the form of a ring in a lion's mouth, cast in the second half of the twelfth century. Legend has it that it was the sanctuary ring that Wenceslas was clinging to when murdered. The figurative corbels of the portal have interesting iconography. On the first of them, the Devil is ripping out Judas' tongue, which symbolizes the road to Hell; on the other corbel, referring to the difficult road to the Kingdom of Heaven, St Peter is depicted denying Christ. The Wenceslas Chapel is adorned with wall paintings from two periods. In the lower register on all four walls of the chapel are wall paintings with the subject of the Passion and the Glory: the Agony in the Garden, the Betrayal, Christ before Pilate, the Flagellation, the Crown of Thorns, the Crucifixion, the Lamentation, the Resurrection, the Ascension, and the Decent of the Holy Spirit. As the path to salvation, the Crucifixion is symbolically placed in the centre of the altar wall. Christ on the Cross is being worshiped by Charles IV and

Elizabeth of Pomerania, his fourth wife, and Wenceslas IV and Joanna of Bavaria, his first wife. The scenes of the Flagellation and the Crown of Thorns assume the character of independent devotional images, which is probably connected with relics of the Passion. The paintings were made *c*.1372, and are ascribed to Master Oswald. In 1372–73, the walls of the chapel with the cycle of paintings were encrusted with gemstones similarly to the Chapel of the Holy Cross at Karlstein Castle (see below). Because of its square plan and the gem-encrusted walls, the Wenceslas Chapel is considered a prefiguration of the Heavenly Jerusalem.

A splendid tombstone of St Wenceslas originally dominated the chapel. From the cathedral inventory of 1387, we know that it looked like a reliquary shrine and stood in the middle of the south wall on an oblong pedestal. Abutting the back of the shine was the altar slab on which there was a golden herma with the skull of St Wenceslas. The east side of the tomb was magnificently decorated: below were busts of the Emperor Charles IV and his third wife Anne of Schweidnitz, in sculpted relief in sardonyx (a valuable kind of onyx with red bands instead of black). They wore golden crowns set with pearls and gemstones.

In relief, in the middle of the front side, was the figure of St Wenceslas. In his right hand he clutched his lance on which was a pennon bearing the eagle of St Wenceslas, and in his left hand he held a shield bearing a lion made of pearls. The corbel on which the saint stood was in the shape of a crown set with rubies, sapphires, and pearls. Wenceslas's cuirass was decorated with cameos, and, in the middle, was a splendid reliquary, probably in the form of the clasp of his cloak. On his head, St Wenceslas wore a crown of gold set with gemstones and pearls. In the upper part of the front of the tomb, the Dextera Domini (the right hand of God) was emerging from the clouds and blessing St Wenceslas and the royal couple. God was wearing a diamond ring, and the hem of Wenceslas's robe was decorated with cameos. The Dextera Domini was accompanied by two angels. Above it was a ring, a large emerald, and a reliquary containing a human skull. The edge of the front of the tomb was adorned with three rows of cameos and the entire front surface was decorated with cameos and gemstones. Below the busts of the king and queen were five little crosses set with pearls and cameos.

On one of the longitudinal sides of the tomb were eighteen panels decorated in relief and arranged in three rows of six. In the first, at the top, from the left, were panels portraying St Paul, St Peter, Christ, the Virgin, a reliquary panel with the hair of the Virgin and depiction of St Mark being adored by Charles IV and an unidentified patriarch. The last panel had portraits of Sts Luke, Matthew, and John. In the second row, from the left, were reliefs portraying Sts Vitus, Adalbert, and Wenceslas, a golden cross with two angels, St Ludmila and St Benedict and Companions (Benedictines, also known as the Five Polish Brothers – Benedict, with John, Matthew, Isaac, and Christinus, who went with Adalbert on a mission to the pagan Slavs). In the lower row were portrayed the martyrdoms of Vitus, Adalbert, and Wenceslas. On the fourth panel, from the left, was a Nativity scene. On the fifth was the martyrdom of Ludmila and on the last were the martyrdoms of Benedict and Companions. The upper part of the tomb had a horizontal lid with a roof-like shelter. A side of the lid was adorned with 45 different cameos and a small gold cross. The little roof was covered with golden panels, and below were portraits of Ernest of Pardubice (Bishop of Prague), Albert of Sternberg (Bishop of

Olomouc), John of Luxembourg (Bishop of Strasbourg), and six other lords with their coats of arms. The opposite side was without decoration, because in front of it stood the cross and candelabra. From the weekly accounts of the lodge we may deduce that the tombstone was protected by a grille. The tomb would be opened for distinguished guests of the court, who were shown the relics of Wenceslas, the then principal Bohemian patron saint. The splendid tombstone was plundered mostly by the Emperor Sigismund in 1414, the year he was crowned King of the Romans (that is, King of the Germans). To obtain the funds to pay his soldiers, he removed fourteen panels from its side and the golden plaques from its roof. The remainder of the decoration was then taken, on 30 July 1420, to Karlstein for safekeeping. During the Hussite siege of the castle in 1422, the front part of the tomb was dismantled and the gold was then sold.

The original furnishings of the St Wenceslas Chapel included a metalwork tower bearing the Imperial and Bohemian coats of arms. Located in the south-east corner of the chapel, it originally served as a Sacrament house. From the accounts of Prague Cathedral we know it was made by a lodge smith called Wenceslas in 1375. The altar slab in the chapel is medieval and comes from the Chapel of St Anne, as is evident from the damaged relief of the Virgin and Child with St Anne.

Some of the other chapels also contain fragments of medieval decoration. Apart from the Wenceslas Chapel, the best-preserved original medieval decoration is in the Chapel of Sts Erhard and Odilia (also known as the Vlašim Chapel or the Chapel of the Visitation). Founded by the Archbishop of Prague, John Očko of Vlašim, it was also meant to be his burial chapel. The archbishop's body lies in the tomb, which is adorned with a recumbent effigy of him with a dog at his feet. Unlike the tombs of the dukes and kings in the choir chapels, the figurative part of this tomb is carved of very hard siliceous rock. On the wall above it are the coats of arms of Očko and the lords of Vlašim and Jenstein. In 1367, Očko ordered and funded there an altar dedicated to Sts Erhard and Odilia. In about 1367, the chapel walls were covered with wall paintings. On the east wall is a scene of the Baptism of St Odilia, the patroness of people suffering from eye ailments. Očko, who suffered from glaucoma of the right eye, prayed to her for help. The relics of Odilia, together with those of Erhard, were acquired for the Treasury of St Vitus' Cathedral by Charles IV in 1365. The other painting in the chapel portrays Očko venerating the Man of Sorrows holding a cross (Christus Victor) and Adalbert, the patron saint of the archdiocese. The composition includes the subject of the Beheading of St Catherine.

The Chapel of St Mary Magdalene, on the south side of the choir, also contains wall paintings from this period. It was finished in late 1369. Its dedication to Mary Magdalene may be connected to the fact that in 1365 (and then again in 1370) Charles IV received relics of this saint in the kingdom of Arles (also called the Second Kingdom of Burgundy). The devotional wall painting of the Virgin with St Mary Magdalene, St James the Great, other saints, and two kneeling canons was made c.1370. The tombstones of the master masons of the medieval choir, Matthew of Arras and Peter Parler, are set into the chapel walls. Other choir chapels were also given costly decoration. In February 1368, to mark the birth of his son Sigismund, the Emperor Charles IV, as Benedict Krabice of Weitmühle writes, had the Chapel of St Sigismund 'remarkably decorated with gold and silver, and donated 1,000 ducats on the day of the boy's baptism as a fee for the preservation of this altar'.

Benedict Krabice of Weitmühle (Beneš Krabice z Veitmile)

This chronicler of Charles's court came from an old Bohemian family of the lower nobility, which originated in Thüringen. Little is known about his education, but it is assumed that he graduated from Prague University and, in 1359, became a canon of the St Vitus' Chapter. In 1355, Benedict became the third Clerk of the Works of St Vitus' Cathedral. He implemented Charles's idea to translate the relics of the Přemyslid dukes and kings to the choir chapels of the cathedral and bury them in tombs decorated with effigies. It was also thanks to him that the mortal remains of the bishops of Prague were translated to the cathedral choir. He wrote a four-volume chronicle of the period during the reign of Charles IV, and, at the emperor's command, he included Charles's autobiography and the biography of Ernest of Pardubice in the fourth volume.

Charles IV had the body of Sigismund, a new patron saint of Bohemia whose relics he had brought here from St Moritz in 1365, buried in the chapel.

The tombs of the patron saints of Bohemia form an emblematic cross in the cathedral: in the choir are the relics of St Vitus; on the right, in the Wenceslas Chapel, is the tomb of St Wenceslas; in the chapel on the left is the body of St Sigismund; the tomb of St Adalbert was supposed to be in the nave; and the area in the middle of this cross was reserved for the royal crypt with a place for Charles IV.

On his travels, Charles acquired a great many relics for the cathedral. He then had Prague artisans make precious reliquaries for them. Thus, the Treasury of St Vitus' experienced its greatest prosperity during the reign of Charles IV. The beginnings of the treasury date from the reign of the first Přemyslids, in the tenth century, when Wenceslas I, Duke of Bohemia, received a relic, a bone of St Vitus', as a gift from Henry the Fowler, King of Germany.

By the end of the Přemyslid dynasty several dozen important objects had been collected, most of which, however, have since been gradually stolen. Thanks to several preserved cathedral inventories from the reign of Charles IV, it is possible to trace the progressive enlargement of the treasury. The inventory for 1354 contains 316 items; a year later it had 413, and in 1374 the number had grown to 542. Of the items from Charles's period, we would mention the magnificent cross of the kingdom of Bohemia, the cross of Pope Urban V, an onyx chalice, a rock-crystal ewer for a fragment of the tablecloth from the Last Supper, reliquary busts of the patron saints of Bohemia (later stolen by the Emperor Sigismund). Of the earlier relics preserved in the Treasury of St Vitus', one should mention not only those of St Wenceslas (his helmet, chain-mail shirt, and sword), but also the crosier and mitre of St Adalbert. Although there were as many as ninety altars in the cathedral choir at the end of the fourteenth century, very few panel paintings have been preserved.

Construction work on the cathedral continued until the Hussite Wars (1419–c.1434). Afterwards, the efforts of the Jagiellons and Habsburgs to finish the cathedral were in vain. Not even the legend that the ruler who completed the cathedral would vanquish the Turk helped them to complete the task. Not until 1859 was the Society for the Completion of St Vitus's Cathedral (Jednota pro dostavbu svatovítského dómu) established. Two years later, the architect Joseph Kranner began the restoration of the early part of the cathedral. After Kranner's death, the architect Josef Mocker took over the work, but even he did not succeed in finishing the work before he died in 1899. That task was left for Kamil Hilbert. The finished cathedral was re-consecrated to mark the millennium of the death of St Wenceslas in 1929.

In 1346, thanks to the favour showed him by Pope Clement VI and his own powerful relations, including Baldwin of Luxembourg, the Archbishop-Elector of Trier, Charles IV was elected King of the Romans in the town of Rhens on the Rhine. He was crowned in Bonn, because Aix-la-Chapelle (today's Aachen), the traditional place for the coronation of the Kings of the Romans, supported the Emperor Louis IV, the Bavarian. In that same year, John of Luxembourg, King of Bohemia, now completely blind, died at the Battle of Crécy. Consequently, Charles, after having ruled together with his father, became the King of Bohemia. The coronation was held at Prague Castle on 2 September of the following year, now with a new crown, which Charles had ordered made in 1344–45 and had dedicated to St Wenceslas. The crown was supposedly kept for a whole year on a golden herma with the skull of Duke Wenceslas, which was placed on Wenceslas's tomb. It was probably after the destruction of the tomb and the herma of St Wenceslas during the Hussite Wars that the crown was moved to the Crown Chamber, located above the Chapel of St Wenceslas. The entrance to the Crown Chamber, remodelled during the reconstruction of the cathedral in the nineteenth century, is directly from the Wenceslas Chapel, through a door with seven locks. Today, seven officials hold the keys to those locks. This tradition is quite recent, going back only to the end of the eighteenth century. At the request of the Bohemian Estates, the Emperor Leopold II, in 1792, established the Office of the Keepers of the Crown Jewels. There were two keepers, one from the nobility, one from the gentry. They were obliged to take an oath of allegiance to the Governor of Bohemia and the Lord High Burgrave, the latter of whom subsequently handed each of them their own individual keys. In the course of the nineteenth and twentieth centuries, the structure of the keepers of the keys changed with the state administration and the régime.

In the years 1346 to 1348 Charles made some of his most important donations in Prague, including the founding of Prague University, which was approved by the Bohemian Diet on 7 April 1348. Efforts to found the university had been made before him by Wenceslas II, but also met with the resistance of the Bohemian nobility.

Charles, by the Grace of God, King of the Romans semper augustus, and King of Bohemia. To serve as a permanent record of the matter.

Among the desires of our heart and that which continuously occupies our royal mind with its weightiness, the heed, concern and attention of our mind is constantly turning to our desire that the Bohemian kingdom – which we love above all our other honourable acquisitions and possessions, be they hereditary or acquired by good fortune, with the special affection of our mind, and for whose ennoblement we strive with all our great ardour and for whose honour and good we strive with all our efforts – should, as by act of God, rejoice in the natural plenitude of the fruits of the earth, and should be adorned, by the order of our providence and our endeavour in our time, with a multitude of learned men.

And thus that our loyal people of the kingdom, who crave with unceasing hunger for the fruit of learning, should not need to beg for alms in foreign lands, but should find in our kingdom a table laid for feasting, and that those who are distinguished by their acuity, both innate and given from above, should become educated through the acquisition of knowledge, and should no longer be forced to wander around the world, turn to foreign nations, or to beg in alien parts in order to quench their craving, now considering such wandering useless, but that they should instead consider it their honour to be able to invite others from foreign lands and let them partake of that delectable fragrance and great gratitude.

Therefore, in order for such beneficial and praiseworthy intentions of our mind to bear dignified fruit and for the dignity of our kingdom to be multiplied by pleasing new deeds, on having prudently contemplated the matter we have decided to establish, elevate and newly create a *Studium generale* in our metropolitan and especially charming town of Prague, abounding in both a wealth of fruits of the earth and amenity of the place, so convenient and suited for such a great task.

At this *Studium generale* there will be doctors, masters and pupils of all faculties, to whom we promise excellent goods, and to those whom we consider deserving thereof, we shall grant royal gifts.

The doctors, masters and pupils at any faculty and beyond, all together and each one separately, no matter whence they hail, whether during their travels, during their stay, or on their return, we wish to keep under special protection and under the aegis of our majesty, giving to them all a solid guarantee that all privileges, prerogatives and freedoms – such as they enjoy by decree of royal power and such as are enjoyed by the doctors and pupils of both the Paris and Bologna *Studia generale* – shall be graciously granted to each and all who may wish to come here, and that we shall ensure that these freedoms be inviolably honoured by each and all.

As evidence thereof, and for safe assurance, we have had this charter drafted and have ordered that it be confirmed by the seal of our majesty. Done in Prague, in the first indiction, on the seventh day of the month of April of the year of Our Lord thirteen hundred and forty eight, in the second year of our rule.

(trans. Anna Bryson)

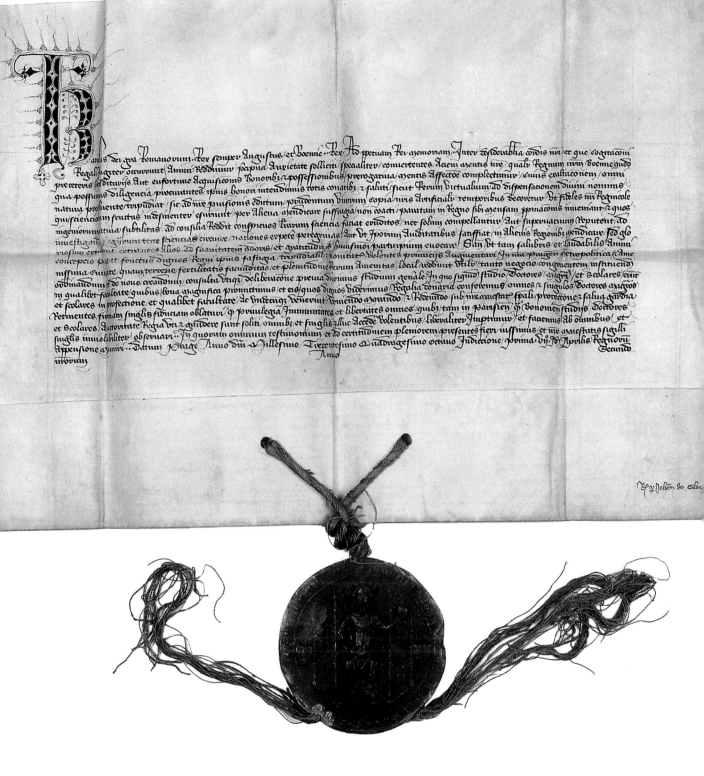

The Foundation Charter of Charles University, Prague

The founding of the University of Prague, the oldest university in central Europe, is among the most important of Charles's foundations. As he wrote in the charter of 7 April 1348, he founded the university 'so that our loyal subjects of the kingdom, who continuously hunger for the fruits of learning do not have to go to foreign countries to beg for alms, but can instead find in our kingdom the table set for feasting [...], so that they consider it their glory that they can invite others from abroad and to make them participants of that delectable fragrance and great gratitude'. In the charter, Charles also guarantees special protection to all students and grants them privileges that they can enjoy thanks to the king's might, which doctors and students at the universities of Paris and Bologna enjoy. Pope Clement VI had, almost a year earlier, supported Charles's intention to found a university in Prague with a document of 26 January 1347.

The Prague University seal: its impression and silver matrix

The seal is a magnificent work of art and the most important symbol of Prague University. The silver matrix was made in the mid-fourteenth century, probably by a Prague goldsmith. It is dominated by the figure of the eternal heir of the Bohemian Lands, the patron saint of the university, Wenceslas, dressed in scale armour, holding a pennon adorned with the letter W. Kneeling on his left is Charles IV, with the foundation charter of the university in his hand, entrusting him with the protection of the University of Prague. The background of this image is decorated with lozenges filled with rosettes. The seal is still used today on the degree and prize certificates granted by Charles University, Prague.

Charles had become acquainted with the university milieu during his sojourn in Paris, where the university had been successfully developing under the aegis of the kings of France. Though he did not study at the University of Paris, he probably did acquire knowledge of theology and philosophy there from his teacher, Pierre Roger, the future Pope Clement VI, and it was to him that Charles, in 1346, sent an embassy with the request to found the University of Prague. The request was supported during negotiations at the Curia in Avignon by the Archbishop of Prague, Ernest of Pardubice. The importance of founding an institution of higher learning was officially stated by Charles in the Golden Bull of 1356, which he issued as the Holy Roman Emperor and King of Bohemia. In this constitutional document, the most important of the medieval empire, he placed the university in the protection of the chief patron saint of Bohemia, Wenceslas. Although this is reflected in the university seal of the fourteenth century, the university was meant to serve the needs not just of the kingdom of Bohemia but of the whole Empire.

For a few years, the university did not have its own building, and lectures were held in monasteries and in rooms linked to St Vitus' Cathedral. But in the 1350s, the colleges began to be established. The first, Caroline College (1366), and subsequent ones, for example, Queen Hedwig College, All Saints' College, and Wenceslas IV College, were founded chiefly to provide board and lodging for the teachers. The university also had its estates (for example, the village of Horní Počernice, on the east edge of Prague), from whose revenues the teachers' stipends and teaching

expenses were paid. Of fundamental importance for the development of Prague University was a gift from Charles's son, Wenceslas IV – namely, the medieval house of the patrician family of Rotlev, which Wenceslas gave to the university after having it rebuilt from 1383 to 1386. It has a chapel with an oriel, part of whose exterior decoration suggests that the Parler lodge may have been involved in its construction. The remodelled house became the centre of university life and the seat of the rector, and has remained so to this day. Until 1945, maces, partly from the Middle Ages, were used at graduations and other university ceremonies.

An important building of Charles's period, linking the Lesser Town with the Old Town of Prague, was the new bridge over the River Vltava, called the Stone Bridge or the Prague Bridge (but Charles Bridge only since 1870), built to take the place of the collapsed Judith Bridge. It was most probably founded on 15 June, that is, the Feast Day of St Vitus, a patron saint of Bohemia, as is suggested by a depiction of the saint on the façade of the Old Town bridge tower, in which Vitus is standing on the bridge (that is to say, it has been placed in his care). There is, however, also a popular view that the bridge was founded on 9 July 1357, at 5.31 a.m., during the favourable conjunction of the Sun and Saturn. This date corresponds to the sequence of odd numbers from one to nine and back, that is, 1–3–5–7–9–7–5–3–1. The bridge, generally believed to have been built by Peter Parler, is roughly 516 metres long, 9.5 metres wide, and rises to a height of 13 metres above the river. It comprises sixteen arches, whose piers were built on oak piles and millstones. The bridge, whose mortar allegedly included egg and wine, was very costly to build, which is why until 1816 a toll was paid to cross it. Since Charles's time there has been a Christian cross on the bridge. In the Late Gothic period a wayside shrine was added, and, on the Lesser Town side, a statue of the legendary knight Bruncvík (Roland) was added as well, a reminder of the privileges and rights that the Old Town had to the bridge.

The Old Town side of the bridge is dominated by the robust and splendidly decorated three-stage bridge tower. Built by Peter Parler and his lodge on the first inner pier of the bridge in the 1370s and 1380s, it is made of ashlars and covered with a roof of slate (originally of gilded lead sheet). The gate through the tower is covered with a distinctive Parler-type triradial vault, with the motif of an open royal crown in the centre. The east and the west side of the tower were originally decorated with sculpture, but the west side was badly damaged during the Swedish siege of the Old Town in 1648 (as is attested by the inscription on the stone plaque). Today, only the decoration on the east side of the tower, reminiscent of a triumphal arch, has been preserved. Above the arch of the gate are the coats of arms of the lands ruled by Charles IV. In the place of honour, on the right-hand side of the pointed Gothic arch, are enthroned the Emperor Charles IV and, on the left, his son Wenceslas IV, King of Bohemia. Between them are two depictions of bridge arches on which, in the middle, stands St Vitus. In the gable above the arch is an escutcheon with the eagle of St Wenceslas. On the third stage are statues of two patron saints of Bohemia, Procopius (?) and Sigismund, with a big lion at their feet. On the west side (which was badly damaged), there was, it is generally believed, a standing figure of the Queen of Heaven (the Woman Clothed in Sun or Woman of the Apocalypse) with the figures of Sts Wenceslas and Adalbert. The lower part of the east façade is decorated with a number of small symbolic statues (for example, a lion fighting with an eagle). Particularly worthy of attention is the repeated emblem of Wenceslas IV– a kingfisher ringed by a torse (a wreath of twisted fabric), which also decorates his manuscripts. Also from his time, perhaps, come the much overpainted wall paintings in the cells of the vaults in the tower gate.

The improving economic conditions in the reign of the Luxembourgs naturally led also to the development of the towns. That is certainly true of the Old Town of Prague, whose centre was, and still is, Old Town Square. Here were the houses of rich burghers, including Stone Bell House, which belonged to King John and Queen Elizabeth. Charles IV was probably born here in 1316. The façade was decorated with statues of John and Elizabeth, and also supporters of escutcheons and perhaps too the patron saints of the Bohemia Lands. This was high-quality sculpture, probably French. The house has two medieval chapels, which are decorated with wall paintings from c.1340. The paintings in the ground-floor chapel depict the Arma Christi (the Instruments of the Passion) and episodes from the Legend of St Wenceslas.

For the economic development of the town, market places and the concomitant privileges granted by the monarch were particularly important. An indispensible role in the town was played by the artisan guilds. During the reign of Charles IV, goldsmiths (whose patron saint is Eligius) and painters (whose patron saint is Luke) added their numbers to the traditional guilds. An expression of the self-confidence of the burghers was local self-government; its seat was the Old Town town hall. The burghers of the Old Town were granted permission to build the town by John of Luxembourg in 1338. The new town hall was erected on foundations of the patrician house of Wolflin of Kamen. The town hall tower was erected on earlier foundations on the east side of the house in the mid-fourteenth century, and made taller in 1364; it was given a bell in 1409. Probably towards the end of the reign of Charles IV a clock was added to its north side, built by a clockmaker called Martin. After 1360, another house was added to the town hall, in which a council chamber and a chapel were built. On the outside of the building a statue of the 'Virgin of the Old Town' was placed under a stone canopy.

The main church of the Old Town of Prague is doubtless the Thein Church (also called the Church of the Virgin before the Thein). It was founded in the 1130s near the Ungelt, an enclosed courtyard for foreign merchants protected by the Crown. The Ungelt (once also called the Thein Yard) contained warehouses, stables, and inns for merchants. In return for royal protection in the Middle Ages, a fee (*umgeld* or *ungelt*), later an excise tax, was collected from the merchants in the Ungelt. The remodelling of the Thein Church began at the west façade in the mid-fourteenth century. By the end of the 1380s, both side aisles and the masonry of the nave had been added. But any plans to finish the roof and vaulting were thwarted by the Hussite Wars. Charles IV's involvement in the building of the church is probably reflected in the sedile of the chapel on the south side of the choir, decorated with stone busts of the king and the queen, carved by the lodge of Matthew of Arras. In the late 1360s and early 1370s the decoration of the north portal began. Later, Wenceslas IV contributed greatly to the decoration of the church, once he had moved his seat from Prague Castle to the more comfortable King's Court, which was located where the Municipal House now stands. Already in the period before the Hussites, the Thein Church was the seat of the movement for Church reform. Here, Conrad Waldhauser, an Augustinian canon, and later Jacobellus of Mies (Jakoubek ze Stříbra) a fellow-reformer and friend of John Huss's, preached here, the latter defending the administration of Communion 'under two kinds', that is, not just the bread but also the wine.

Charles's most important act as a founder was the founding of the New Town of Prague. His motivation was the growing population of Prague, which was now the seat of the King of the Romans and the King of Bohemia. After the founding of the university, many students from foreign countries were coming to Prague, and considerable interest was also shown by pilgrims because Charles was collecting saints' relics from all over Europe and putting them in Prague churches. The intention to expand the capital with the addition of a new borough was announced by Charles seven months after he had come to the throne, and on 26 March 1348, with the participation of his court, he laid the foundation stone of the walls of the New Town. For strategic reasons, he had originally considered the flat terrain on the left bank of the Vltava (at what is today Letná), but ultimately, for reasons of public health – probably on the advice of his astronomer, mathematician, and physician Gall (Havel) – he chose a site on the right bank between the Old Town and Vyšehrad, with better access to water. The land chosen by Charles had already been discontinuously but densely built up. Probably the most important settlement before the founding of the town, then in the lower part of the New Town, was Na Poříčí (that is, Riverside). Individual farmsteads, concentrated around the churches of St Clement and St Peter, lined the road leading from a gate of the Old Town (today's Powder Tower), the farmstead and hospital of St Benedict, and all the way to the Spital Court, that is, Bishop's Court. The existing buildings on this land were to be organically incorporated into the newly founded town. The main roads of the New Town were continuations of those leading from the Old Town gates. The

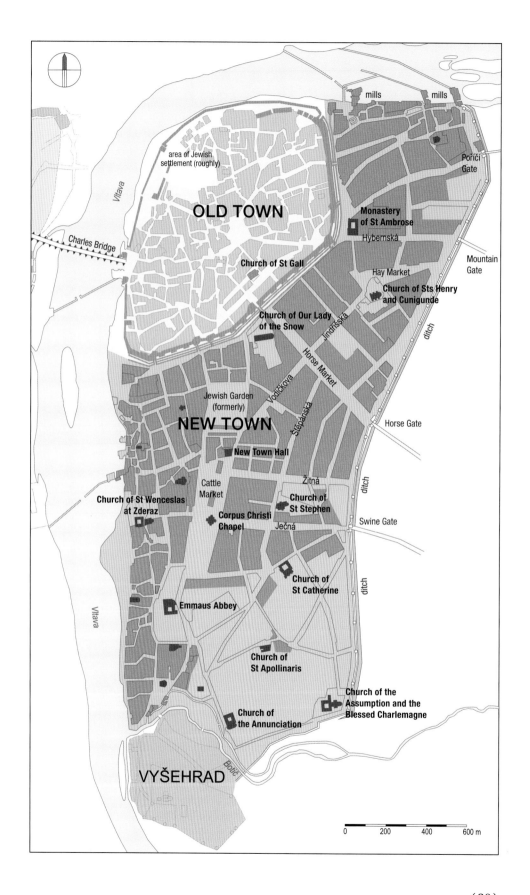

OLD TOWN

NEW TOWN

VYŠEHRAD

Vltava

Vltava

Botič

Charles Bridge

area of Jewish
settlement (roughly)

Monastery
of St Ambrose

Hybernská

Church of St Gall

Hay Market

Church of Sts Henry
and Cunigunde

Church of Our Lady
of the Snow

Jindřišská

Horse Market

Vodičkova

Štěpánská

Jewish Garden
(formerly)

New Town Hall

Cattle
Market

Žitná

Church of St Wenceslas
at Zderaz

Corpus Christi
Chapel

Church of
St Stephen

Ječná

Church of
St Catherine

Emmaus Abbey

Church of
St Apollinaris

Church of the
Assumption and the
Blessed Charlemagne

Church of
the Annunciation

mills

mills

Poříčí
Gate

Mountain
Gate

ditch

Horse Gate

ditch

Swine Gate

ditch

0   200   400   600 m

The New Town of Prague (Nové Město pražské)

Matthew of Arras, the first master mason of St Vitus' Cathedral, is generally considered to be the man behind the urban plan of the New Town of Prague, which was adapted to the terrain and the main existing transport routes. The plan of the New Town comprises two seemingly independent, rectilinearly delimited, interlinked parts.

The south-oriented part is defined by the connecting line running from Staroměstské náměstí (Old Town Square) to Vyšehrad. Upon it was put the largest marketplace of the New Town, the Cattle Market, today's Karlovo náměstí (Charles Square), the basis of the street grid. The main roads were Ječná ulice, originally called Svinská ulice or Svinský trh (named for its intended use, Swine Road or Swine Market), and Žitná ulice (Corn Road). The Swine Market and the Horse Market (today's Wenceslas Square) were joined by Štěpánská ulice (Stephan Street). The north-east tip of the Cattle Market, from where the main connecting line was drawn to the Horse Market, was reserved for the New Town town hall.

The axis of the second unit runs from Old Town Square to St Gall's Market and its area is Wenceslas Square. The grid of streets was developed along both sides of Wenceslas Square, with the main road formed by what are now the streets Vodičkova and Jindřišská. The earliest and largest church buildings of the New Town – Emmaus Abbey and the Church of Our Lady of the Snow – were founded so that each of them marked one of the main axes of the New Town. Some scholars believe that the basic axes of the New Town may have been demarcated from the steeple of St Gall's Church, at which point they precisely intersect. Towards the end of Charles's reign, the north part of the town was intersected by another radial road, formed by the street today called Hybernská. An axis ran through it crosswise: in a south-west direction ran the route to the third New Town market, the Haymarket (today's Senovážné náměstí); from the north side it led to the river.

The conception of the New Town plan is linked to the three main street axes of the Old Town. In an easterly direction, the continuation of Celetná is Hybernská; Jilská continues south to Spálená, and the angle that these streets make is intersected by the axis of Václavské náměstí.

Covering an area of 80,550 square metres, Karlovo náměstí is the largest square in the Czech Republic and one of the largest in Europe. About 130 by 510 metres, it was meant to be the marketplace and centre of the New Town of Prague, established by Charles IV in 1348. Because cattle were sold in its south part, it was originally called the Cattle Market. In the middle of the marketplace stood the Chapel of Corpus Christi, in which pilgrims were shown the most holy relics of the kingdom and, indeed, the empire.

newly founded town had two main parts: the upper New Town, with its centre at the Cattle Market (today's Charles Square, Karlovo náměstí), consisted of basically two other parts: a larger, continuously built-up area to the north-west, stretching from the Old Town walls to the convent of St Catherine and the monastery of Emmaus, and a smaller, more sparsely populated area with vineyards and orchards on the south-east, on the slopes and in the valleys around Větrov and Slup. Near the Old Town was the Horse Market (today's Wenceslas Square) adjacent to Příkopy (the Ditches) and Můstek (the Footbridge, that is, over the ditch). An imaginary dividing line between the upper and the lower New Town was the Carmelite monastery with the Church of Our Lady of the Snow. The centre of the lower New Town was the Hay Market (today's Senovážné náměstí). Among the important roads of this part of town were what are today Hybernská and Na Příkopě streets.

Charles founded the New Town on a grand design. Its central point, the Cattle Market, with an area of eight hectares, is still the largest square in Prague. The roads that led into it were between 23 and 27 metres in width. The town developed quickly thanks particularly to the king's promise that owners of lots who built houses on them within eighteen months would be exempt from all taxes for twelve years. During the first four years, about 600 houses were built here. The grand scale

The Chapel of Corpus Christi (Kaple Božího těla)

A veduta of Prague from 1606, by Philips van den Bossche, Johannes Wechter, and Aegidius Sadeler, shows, in the middle of the Cattle Market, the stone Chapel of Corpus Christi with its high central square steeple. It was built from 1382 to 1393, during the reign of Wenceslas IV, on the site of a wooden towered building erected by Charles IV, in which, every year beginning in 1354 on the Feast of the Holy Lance and Nails, that is, the first Friday after Easter, relics that Charles IV had collected were shown to pilgrims. The displaying of the relics had its own order. First of all, relics connected with Christ were presented. Then came relics linked with the Virgin, followed by relics linked with the patron saints of Bohemia and other saints. From the chapel important decrees were also announced to the congregation; in 1437, for example, the Basle Compactata, a treaty that accepted the Utraquists, was announced here. Until 1610, a procession of mourners went annually from the Carolinum to the chapel to mark the anniversary of the death of Charles IV. The rectors of Prague University were also buried in the chapel. It was demolished during the reforms of Emperor Joseph II (in 1789).

of Charles's foundation is also attested to by the fact that the New Town was not completely built up until the nineteenth century. A reasonable estimate is that the New Town was designed for 50,000 people, who would live in about 5,000 houses, but that was never achieved in the Middle Ages. (At the end of Charles's reign, 40,000 people, living in 3,000 houses, constituted the population of all of Prague.) The most architecturally imposing houses, belonging mostly to merchants, were built on narrow lots near Charles Square. They were made of stone, often in combination with timber framing. Most of the houses each had a ground floor with an arcade facing the square and a large, usually commercial, space (for example, a tap room) called a *Maßhaus* (*mázhaus*, in Czech), taking up the front part of the ground floor. Upstairs is where the family lived. The houses of the richest families each had a private chapel as well. The less expensive houses of the artisans were located in the streets leading to the square. Though Czech was the dominant language in town, there were also communities of German-speaking merchants here, for example, around the Church of St Gall (kostel sv. Havla), and Jews. The grandest building of the town, from the fourteenth century onward, was the town hall, usually in the main square of the borough. At the upper end of the Cattle Market, from 1377 to 1413, the New Town town council built for itself a large and architecturally imposing town hall, which later, at the beginning of the Hussite Revolution, became the scene of the defenestration of its town councillors. The monarch granted the New Town the privileges usual in royal boroughs, for example, the right to hold markets or the right to brew beer, but also the 'mile right', which meant that no foreign artisan, without the permission of the town, could settle within a mile of it), the right of fortification, and the right to pass the death penalty. Near the town, Charles commanded that extensive vineyards be planted.

The main source of revenue for Charles was rich silver mines. Consequently, Kutná Hora (Kuttenberg, in German), where not only silver was mined, but also the famous Prague groschen was minted (a coin widely accepted throughout Europe), became an important city of the kingdom, second only to Prague. Charles's gold ducats were also a much sought-after currency. In financial matters, Charles, like his father, sought the counsel of Florentine and Sienese bankers. He also endeavoured to support commerce in the Bohemian Lands, because, unlike the rich free imperial cities, the long trade routes did not go through this country. Merchants from Bohemia (Czechs and Germans) were given preferential treatment by Charles at markets in free imperial cities, including exemption from customs and excise duties.

Charles was imprinting the newly established town with a unified spiritual concept, seeking to make it into a 'little Rome'. He invited religious orders and congregations to the new convents and monasteries. By their consecration, each of the newly founded Church buildings reflected Charles's political concepts and aspirations. Within sight of the Old Town, a Carmelite monastery was built with a church dedicated to the same saint as one of the first Marian basilicas in Rome – the Basilica di Santa Maria Maggiore (also known as Basilica di Santa Maria della Neve, the Basilica of Our Lady of the Snow). Permission for the Carmelites to settle in Prague was granted by Pope Clement VI in a charter of 29 March 1346, and Charles founded the monastery on 3 September 1347, the day after his coronation. For the rafters of the monastery church, he donated the wood from the podium on which the coronation banquet had been held. The iconographic programme of the reliefs on the 'tympanum' of the Church of Our Lady of the Snow (kostel Panny Marie Sněžné) clearly reflect Charles's having been crowned King of Bohemia, but these reliefs were originally part of the decoration of the front façade of the great tower of the monastery complex. After the tower was torn down, the reliefs were reused to form a triangular tympanum above the gate to the monastery grounds. This was intended to be the largest church building in the New Town, but only the presbytery was built, and in later centuries it was damaged and reduced in height. The foundations of the nave reach all the way to what is today Jungmannovo náměstí (Jungmann Square).

By founding the monastery of the Slav Benedictines, called Emmaus (Emauzy, and also Na Slovanech), Charles IV wished to continue the tradition of Greater Moravia (c.830s–906/07) and the Slavonic liturgy from the Benedictine abbey at Sázava, just south of Prague. It may also have been intended to recall the relations between Charles IV and Stefan Dušan, the Emperor of the Srbs and Greeks. It is reasonable also to consider it a political message, that is, a reference to the claim that the true inheritor of Greater Moravian statehood was the king of Bohemia, Charles IV. Permission to found a monastery with a Slavonic liturgy was granted, at the request of Charles IV and the Archbishop of Prague Ernest of Pardubice, by Pope Clement VI on 9 May 1346. Charles issued his own charter of foundation on 21 November 1347. Monks were brought to Prague from the Benedictine abbey of Sts Cosmas and Damian on the island of Pašman, Dalmatia. The abbey with the church (in the form of a three-aisled hall with a narrow presbytery) was built on a rocky knoll above the river. Of the original medieval decoration, the sedile with the coats of arms of Bohemia and the Empire have been preserved, together with fragments of wall paintings. Attached to the church is the abbey cloister with the Imperial Chapel. The wall paintings of the cloister were made in the 1360s and 1370s by artists from the court circle, who had already worked for Charles IV at Karlstein. The concept of the wall decoration of the cloister is based on typology, that is, finding echoes of the Old Testament in the New. The painting of the so-called Emmaus

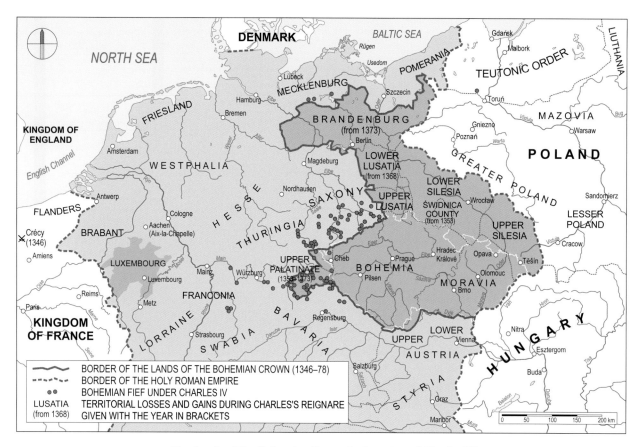

Map labels (clockwise / as positioned):

DENMARK · BALTIC SEA · NORTH SEA · Rügen · Gdańsk · Malbork · LIUTHANIA · Lübeck · Usedom · POMERANIA · Szczecin · TEUTONIC ORDER · Toruń · MECKLENBURG · Hamburg · Bremen · BRANDENBURG (from 1373) · MAZOVIA · Warsaw · FRIESLAND · Berlin · Gniezno · Poznań · POLAND · KINGDOM OF ENGLAND · Amsterdam · Magdeburg · LOWER LUSATIA (from 1368) · GREATER POLAND · WESTPHALIA · Nordhausen · SAXONY · UPPER LUSATIA · LOWER SILESIA · Wrocław · Sandomierz · Antwerp · HESSE · ŚWIDNICA COUNTY (from 1353) · FLANDERS · Cologne · Aachen (Aix-la-Chapelle) · THURINGIA · UPPER SILESIA · LESSER POLAND · Crécy (1346) · BRABANT · Cheb · BOHEMIA · Hradec Králové · Opava · Těšín · Cracow · Amiens · Prague · LUXEMBOURG · Mainz · Würzburg · UPPER PALATINATE (1353–1373) · Pilsen · Olomouc · Luxembourg · Paris · Reims · FRANCONIA · MORAVIA · Brno · Metz · Strasbourg · BAVARIA · Regensburg · LOWER · Nitra · HUNGARY · KINGDOM OF FRANCE · LORRAINE · SWABIA · Danube · Isar · UPPER AUSTRIA · Vienna · Esztergom · Salzburg · Buda · STYRIA · Graz · Maribor

Legend

∿∿∿	BORDER OF THE LANDS OF THE BOHEMIAN CROWN (1346–78)
-----	BORDER OF THE HOLY ROMAN EMPIRE
●●	BOHEMIAN FIEF UNDER CHARLES IV
LUSATIA (from 1368)	TERRITORIAL LOSSES AND GAINS DURING CHARLES'S REIGNARE GIVEN WITH THE YEAR IN BRACKETS

0   50   100   150   200 km

The Lands of the Bohemian Crown in the reign of Charles IV

The Lands of the Bohemian Crown have a long history. After the fall of the Empire of Greater Moravia in *c.*907, the Margravate of Moravia was incorporated into a union with Bohemia, which, in 1137, was joined by the County of Kladsko (Hrabstwo Kłodzkie or Ziemia Kłodzka, in Polish, and Grafschaft Glatz, in German). John of Luxembourg, King of Bohemia, added Upper Lusatia in 1319, Egerland (Chebsko, in Czech) in 1322, and Silesian duchies from 1327 to 1335. Charles IV further increased Bohemia by incorporating other Silesian duchies, the Upper Palatinate (Oberfalz) in 1353, Lower Lusatia in 1368, united as New Bohemia (Nové Čechy) until 1373, and, lastly, Brandenburg in 1373 (which was retained until 1415). The name Lands of the Bohemian Crown was first used by Charles IV in documents in 1348, which were then compiled as the book of Bohemian law.

Crucifixion, made after 1365 under the influence of Theodoric's works, probably comes from the Imperial Chapel. The Emmaus Abbey also had a large illuminators' workshop, from which comes, among other things, the Reims Gospel (also known as the *Texte du Sacre*), on which the kings of France in the early modern period took their oaths during their coronation at Reims. The abbey survived the Hussite Wars almost intact, because the monks received Holy Communion under two kinds.

Another important medieval building of the New Town was the Church of the Assumption and the Blessed Charlemagne (kostel Nanebevzetí Panny Marie a sv. Karla Velikého) at Karlov, where the canonry of the Canons Regular of St. Augustine was established. The church and its abbey were built from 1350 to 1357. The church has a narrow presbytery and a central octagonal nave, which, by its plan, makes reference to the Cathedral at Aix-la-Chapelle, where the Emperor Charlemagne is buried and the kings of the Romans, including Charles IV, were crowned.

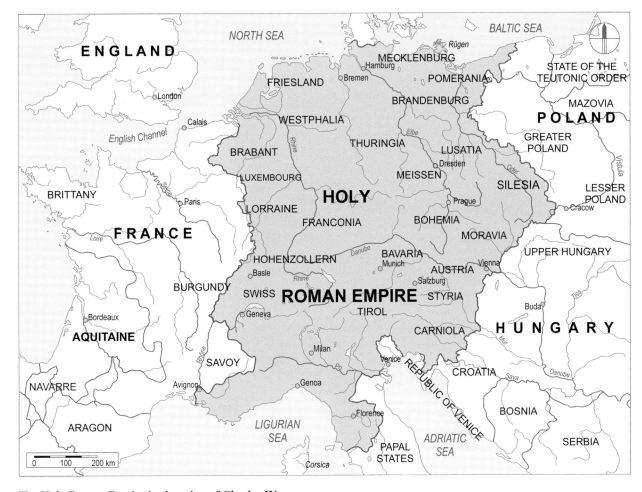

The Holy Roman Empire in the reign of Charles IV

During the reign of Charles IV, the Holy Roman Empire (established in the ninth century) comprised not only what is today Germany and the Czech Republic but also a considerable part of the Low Countries, Luxembourg, Swiss cantons, the Austrian lands, Slovenia, the erstwhile Hinterpommern (Further or Eastern Pomerania) and the Neumark (New March), northern Italy (Lombardy, the Duchy of Friuli), Alsace, Lorraine, part of Burgundy (the Kingdom of Arles), and the southern provinces of the Kingdom of Denmark. The Empire was officially dissolved on 6 August 1806, when its last emperor, Francis II, abdicated after being defeated by Napoleon in the Battle of Austerlitz.

On the hill called Větrov, not far from the Church of the Assumption and the Blessed Charlemagne, is the collegiate Church of St Apollinaris. After an agreement between Charles IV and Ernest of Pardubice in 1362, the canonry was moved here from Sadská, which is just east of Prague. The hall church with a presbytery and a tower on the south side was built from 1360 to 1376. The walls of the nave are decorated with remarkable medieval paintings, which are partly preserved. The tower, 42 metres high, octagonal at its peak, is a landmark of the New Town of Prague. With the founding of the Church of St Catherine as part of the Augustinian nunnery in 1355, Charles IV wanted to commemorate his victory at the Battle of San Felice on St Catherine's Day in 1332, after which he had been dubbed a knight. The church was consecrated by the second Archbishop of Prague, John Očko of Vlašim. To the Church of Our Lady of Humility (kostel Panny Marie Pokorné, also known as Panny Marie Na Slupi), which he ordered built below Vyšehrad, he summoned members of the Servite Order, which had been established at the initiative of Florentine merchants. From this church probably comes the magnificent panel painting of the Madonna dell'Umiltà from *c.*1360. About two centuries later, during the reign of the Emperor Rudolph II, the painting ended up in the Basilica of Sts Peter and Paul at Vyšehrad, and became generally known as the *Vyšehrad Madonna* or the *Madonna of the Rain*.

Charles originally intended to link the Old Town to the New Town, but the former was to be given priority, not merely amongst the towns of Prague, but throughout the country. The Old Town was meant to be the seat of the monarch and therefore the most beautiful. Consequently, artisan workshops, which were too loud or too smelly or both, were to be moved to the New Town. In December 1367, Charles IV ordered the merger of the Old Town and the New Town; in some places, the town walls were therefore demolished, but ten years later, when disputes arose in the administratively joined boroughs, the towns were separated again.

Outside the market places, but still in the heart of the new continuously built-up areas of the lower and the upper town, places were reserved for two new parish churches that played an important role in the town. The first was dedicated to Sts Henry and Cunigunde, the second to St Stephen. Charles greatly venerated Stephen, the Protomartyr of Christianity, and also owned relics of his. The dedication of the church to Sts Henry and Cunigunde may refer to the fact that in the reign of Charles the archbishops of Prague were visiting bishops of the Bamberg diocese, whose patron saints were the Emperor Henry II and his wife Cunigunde of Luxembourg. Building work on both churches began in 1351, when their parish boundaries were also set. The old settlements in the New Town, however, remained subordinated to the existing parishes, of which there were nine in all. In the first phase of work, from 1348 to 1353, about 650 burgher houses were built in the area between the Church of Sts Henry and Cunigunde and the Church of St Catherine. On the periphery of the settlements Poříč and at Na Slupi building work began only later, and towards the end of the century it slowed down altogether.

Within two years, the New Town was surrounded by walls almost 3.5 km long and 10 metres high. They included 21 towers built in the wall and four gates, of which the Špička Gate, enabling access to the Horse Market, was particularly impressive. The walls, which enclosed an area of more than 2.4 square kilometres, were not torn down until the last quarter of the nineteenth century. To reinforce the defences of Prague Castle and the Lesser Town, the 'Hunger Wall' (Hladová zeď, as it has been known for years) was built on Petřín Hill, on the orders of the king, from 1360 to 1362. Six metres high and two metres wide, and with eight bastions, it snaked along the west edge of Strahov Abbey, by the Church of St Lawrence (kostel sv. Vavřince) on Petřín Hill, and from there down to the River Vltava. It thus in fact incorporated the now defunct village of Újezd and part of town known as Strahov into the Prague fortifications. At the end of the Hunger Wall stood the Újezd Gate (originally called the Kartouzská brána – Charter House Gate).

Charles's dispute with the Emperor Louis IV the Bavarian, which threatened to escalate into open war, was resolved by the emperor's sudden death in 1347. But that did not end Charles's problems in the Empire, and partisans of the house of Wittelsbach, including Rudolph II, Count Palatine of the Rhine, successfully pushed through the election of Günther von Schwarzburg instead of Charles. But in 1348,

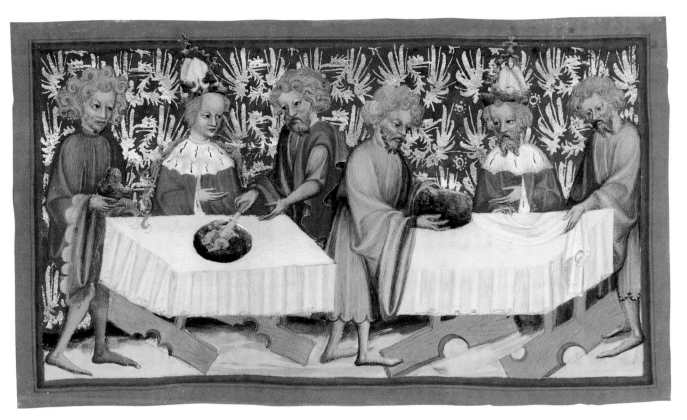

The Golden Bull
Official banquet of the emperor and the empress,
and seal of the Golden Bull

The Golden Bull of Charles IV is among the most important
constitutional documents of the Holy Roman Empire. Each of the
seven Electors received a copy of it. Its regulations were in force
practically to the end of the Empire in 1806. It is called Golden because
the golden seal of the Emperor and King Charles IV was attached
to it (pictured right). The first part of the bull was announced at the
Imperial Diet in Nuremberg at the beginning of 1356, the second part
at Metz in late 1356 and early 1357. The bull laid down the rules for the
election of the King of the Romans, declaring that it would be held in
Frankfurt am Main, that the city of the coronation would be Aix-la-
Chapelle (though Rome would continue to be the city for imperial
coronations), and that the emperor would summon the first Imperial
Diet in Nuremberg. The pope retained only the right to crown the
king, and lost the right to approve the election results. The bull also
contains the regulation that the college of electors should meet once a
year to consult with the emperor. The rank of elector was declared to be
hereditary, and (in addition to Latin) Czech, German, and Italian were
decreed the official languages of the Empire.

after the death of Blanche, Charles asked Rudolph if he would give him his daughter Anne to wed. Rudolph granted his request. Charles also reached an agreement with the ailing Günther that for a fee he would waive all his claims. Afterwards, in June 1349, Charles IV could be received at an assembly of electors and princes of the empire in Frankfurt am Main. Then, a month later, he was crowned King of the Romans at Aix-la-Chapelle. The road to the imperial crown was now open to him.

The dream of Charles IV in Terenzo, from the *Vita Caroli* (Ch. VII)

This particular manuscript of Charles's autobiography was made in Prague in 1472, probably commissioned by King Wladislas II (also known as Ladislas Jagiellon and, in Czech, Vladislav Jagellonský), who in this way sought to demonstrate that his reign followed on from that of Charles IV. Unlike other preserved, sparsely illuminated copies of the *Vita*, each chapter of this manuscript is illustrated.

That night, after we had fallen asleep, we had a dream. An angel of the Lord stood by our bed and struck us on the left side, saying: 'Rise, and come with us!' And we in spirit responded: 'My Lord, I know neither where nor how I would go with you.' And he, seizing us by the topknot, carried us up into the air to a large number of armed knights who stood ready for battle in front of a castle. And he held us in the air above the host and told us: 'Look and see!' And behold, another angel, descending from heaven and holding a fiery sword, struck at one in the midst of the host, and with his sword cut off his genitals, and that man seemed to be mortally wounded and dying on his horse. Then, still holding us by the hair, the angel said: 'Do you know the one who was struck by the angel and put to death?' And we said: 'My Lord, I do not, nor do I know this place.' He said: 'You ought to know that this is the Dauphin of Viennois, who, for the sin of lust, has thus been struck down by God. Now take heed therefore, and you may tell your father to avoid similar sins, or worse things will befall you.'

In January 1350, Charles's second wife, Anne of Bavaria (also of the Palatinate), gave birth to a son, Wenceslas, but the child died less than two years later, and shortly afterwards Anne died too. Following his new marriage, to Anne of Schweidnitz, in Buda, in May 1353, Charles added Upper and Lower Lusatia to the Lands of the Bohemian Crown. In Nuremberg, in 1361, Anne gave birth to Charles's long-awaited heir. He too was given the name Wenceslas. In two years, despite the resistance of Archbishop Ernest, Charles had Wenceslas crowned King of Bohemia. In 1362, Queen Anne died. A year later, Charles married for the fourth time, taking Elizabeth of Pomerania to be his wife. She gave him a son, Sigismund (Zikmund).

After the death of Charles's ally Clement VI, in 1352, Innocent VI became pope. Charles succeeded in obtaining Innocent's consent for his coronation in Rome. After protracted negotiations, the heirs of Louis IV gave the imperial regalia to Charles. On the Feast of St Wenceslas, on 28 September 1354, Charles and his court set out for Rome. They first stopped in Milan, where, on 6 January 1355, the Iron Crown of Lombardy was placed on his head. Charles then went to Pisa, where he was soon joined by his wife, Queen Anne, Archbishop Ernest, and about 4,000 horsemen from Bohemia and elsewhere in the Empire. They remained in Pisa until February, and arrived in Rome on 2 April 1355. Because he had promised the pope that he would spend only a limited amount of time in Rome, Charles set out on the night before the coronation. Disguised as an ordinary pilgrim, he visited the main basilicas of Rome and knelt by the many relics in them. The impressive procession rode through Rome, and Charles was led to St Peter's Basilica, where, during High Mass on 5 April 1355, he was crowned Emperor of the Holy Roman Empire. Queen Anne also received the crown. The Emperor Charles took devotional images of the *vera icon* (Veil of Veronica) and of the Santa Maria di Aracoeli (St Mary of the Altar of Heaven) to Prague with him.

Once he had buttressed his power as emperor, with the help of Rudolph, the Duke of Saxony, and his chancellor, John of Neumarkt, Charles drafted the articles in accordance with which the election of the King of the Romans should be held. The 23 introductory articles of the new code were approved by the Imperial Diet in Nuremberg on 10 January 1356, and another seven articles were approved eleven months later at the diet in Metz on Christmas Day 1356. The collection of articles became generally known as the Golden Bull of the Emperor Charles IV, and became the standard law book of the Empire, in force until 1806, when the Holy Roman Empire ceased to exist. In the Golden Bull it was stipulated that the King of the Romans would be elected by seven Electors: three lords spiritual (the archbishops of Trier, Cologne, and Mainz), and four lords temporal (the king of Bohemia, the Count Palatine of the Rhine, the Duke of Saxony, and the Margrave of Brandenburg). The foremost place among the temporal electors was reserved for the king of Bohemia, who in sessions of the Imperial Diet and at imperial ceremonies had priority over the kings who were present. According to the Golden Bull, in the event of the extinction of a dynasty the Bohemian Diet had the right to freely elect a new king and, last but not least, the kingdom of Bohemia could not be given in fief by the Emperor.

Unfortunately, Charles IV's legal code for Bohemia, which much later came to be known as the *Maiestas Carolina*, never gained general acceptance. In this document, comprising 109 articles, the emperor, together with his advisers, sought to codify the extent of royal privileges, the economic foundation of the throne. That, however, would have limited the rights, whether real or assumed, of the nobles. To the king was also reserved the right to punish misconduct by the nobles. The legal code also distinguished between civil and criminal law, and guaranteed the protection of the forests and the security of the Bohemian Lands. The drafting of the legal code had begun in the early 1350s, but at the general Bohemian Diet in 1355 the nobles rejected it, and Charles IV, who did not want to enter into a dispute with them, annulled the code in an unusual way: in order not to lose face, he declared that the manuscript had been accidently burnt. Another important legal

Ernest of Pardubice

The last Bishop and first Archbishop of Prague, Ernest came from the family of the Lords of Pardubice. He first met Charles IV while at university in Italy and remained among his closest friends for the rest of his life. After the death of John of Dražice, Ernest was appointed Bishop of Prague and a year later Archbishop. He was also the first Chancellor of Prague University. The king often entrusted him with diplomatic negotiations, particularly with the Avignon papal Curia. Like Charles IV, he was a generous patron of the arts.

document of Charles's reign is the *Ordo iudicii terrae*, describing procedural law as used in Bohemian common law, but it also concerned property and criminal law.

Great men know the art of being able to choose excellent colleagues and inspiring friends, and Charles definitely knew how to do that, as is evident from the testimony of the great Italian poet Petrarch, who in one of his letters wrote: 'I do declare that I have never found an environment less barbaric and more affected by humanism than that of the emperor and the several outstanding men around him, whose names I shall refrain from mentioning; they are truly excellent, educated men who in that respect deserve to be better remembered, of manners so fine and pleasant as if they had been born in Attica.'

A model for Charles in his youth may have been his uncle, Baldwin of Luxembourg. Baldwin read theology and canon law at Paris and at the age of only 22 was elected Archbishop of Trier. He thus became one of the most influential men of the Empire and was largely responsible for the election of his elder brother, Henry, and later also Charles IV, as King of the Romans. Baldwin was also an important patron of the arts, as is evinced by the stone bridges in Koblenz and Trier, the magnificent church in Oberwesel with its valuable altarpiece, and the *Codex Balduini Trevirensis*, a remarkable manuscript that in detail relates events of Henry of Luxembourg's journey to Rome and the marriage of John of Luxembourg and Elizabeth of Bohemia.

Charles's personality was shaped in his youth by his French tutor, Pierre Roger, who later became Pope Clement VI. While still a student of theology at the University of Paris, Pierre Roger became known as a true scholar. Owing to his great learning, he was summoned to the court of Philip VI, King of France, and became a member of the privy council. In 1330, at the king's command, he became the tutor

John Očko of Vlašim

After returning from his studies in Italy, John Očko of Vlašim was the provost of the chapter at the Collegiate Church of All Saints at Prague Castle, and was later Bishop of Olomouc. He was also an adviser to Charles IV, and Charles entrusted him with the education of his son, Wenceslas. At the wishes of Charles IV, John, after the death of Ernest of Pardubice, was appointed Archbishop of Prague, and in Charles IV's absence he represented the King of Bohemia in matters related to the Kingdom. He was not against Church reform, and had a social conscience, as is attested, for example, by his founding of hospitals in Prague and Rome. He was a patron of the arts and his activity as a donor is also evident in the archbishop's residence in Roudnice nad Labem.

John of Jenstein

John of Jenstein came from the illustrious line of the lords of Vlašim and Jenstein. His uncle was the second archbishop of Prague, John Očko of Vlašim. Attended the universities of Bologna, Padua, Montpellier, and Paris. In 1373 he became royal chancellor; in 1375, he was appointed Bishop of Meissen, and, in 1379, Archbishop of Prague. The initially good relations with the king, now Wenceslas IV, soured after 1384. Their disagreements came to a peak in 1393 with the torturing to death of Jenstein's vicar general, John Nepomucene. In 1395, he resigned as archbishop, and died in Rome five years later. He is buried in the Basilica di Santa Prassede all'Esquillino. He was a distinguished member of the clergy, and his ideas also inspired the sculptors and painters in the style now known as International Gothic (also called the *Weicher Stil* or *der Schöne Stil*). John of Jenstein was also a prolific writer of theological and literary works.

Votive Panel of John Očko of Vlašim

The painting was probably commissioned by John Očko of Vlašim for the chapel at the bishop's castle in Roudnice nad Labem, which he built. The chapel was dedicated to the Virgin and the Bohemian patron saints. The panel was painted by someone in the circle of Theodoric of Prague, as is suggested by the faces, but unlike Theodoric's sturdy figures, there is already a clear indication here of making them lighter. The iconography corresponds to the dedication of the chapel and the hierarchical structure of medieval society.

The panel is divided into two registers: in the upper is the Virgin enthroned with the Christ Child on her arm; kneeling on her right, is the Emperor Charles IV, commended by St Sigismund; and on the left is a young King Wenceslas IV with his intercessor, the patron saint of the Kingdom of Bohemia, Wenceslas. In the middle of the lower register is the Archbishop of Prague, John Očko of Vlašim, portrayed in profile and kneeling. He is placing his hands into the hands of the patron saint of the archdiocese of Prague, Adalbert, and, as a sign of intercession, the patron saint of the metropolitan church, Vitus, is putting a hand on his shoulder. The collegium of Bohemian patron saints is completed by Ludmila and Procopius (the founder of the Benedictine monastery in Sázava, 45 km south-east of Prague). The iconographic programme of the panel demonstrates the harmonious relationship between the temporal and the spiritual powers during the reign of Charles IV, a source of the success of his rule.

We know Charles IV's appearance from other paintings as well, for example, in St Vitus' Cathedral, in the Lady Chapel at Karlstein Castle, and from manuscripts, Bohemian and foreign. He is usually portrayed slightly bent forward, which may be a reference to the back injuries he sustained in tournaments in his youth.

to Philip's daughter, Blanche, and the Bohemian prince, Wenceslas (who was soon to be called Charles). The two men became friends, and remained so even after Pierre Roger became Pope in 1342. He had his residence at the papal palace in Avignon, which he had splendidly decorated with wall paintings by renowned Italian painters. He granted the Luxembourgs' request that the Prague diocese be elevated to an archdiocese, and he later supported the election of Charles as King of the Romans as well.

Of all the important figures in the circle of Charles IV, Ernest of Pardubice, the first archbishop of Prague, was probably the closest to the monarch. After schooling at the Benedictine abbey in Braunau (Broumov) (north-east Bohemia, near the Polish border) and in Prague, he set out to the universities of Padua and Bologna, where he read theology and, mainly, canon law. It was in Italy that he made the acquaintance of the future Charles IV. While still a student, Ernest visited Avignon. After his return to Bohemia in 1339, he was ordained to the office of priest and, at the intercession of Charles, became a member of the St Vitus' Chapter. A year later, he was appointed Dean. After the death of the Bishop of Prague, John IV of Dražice, Ernest was elected Bishop, and a year later, in 1344, he was appointed the first Archbishop of Prague. In September 1347, with the new Crown of St Wenceslas, Ernest crowned Charles King of Bohemia and Blanche of Valois Queen of Bohemia. After the University of Prague was founded, Ernest became its chancellor. He also sought reform of Church life, and so, in 1349, promulgated a provincial statute, a code of canon law. Charles entrusted Ernest with numerous diplomatic missions,

(43)

Liber Viaticus.

Domini Johannis.

A miniature from the *Liber viaticus of John of Neumarkt*

This miniature from the splendidly illuminated breviary shows John of Neumarkt, Charles's chancellor, kneeling and worshipping Christ in Majesty. The manuscript of the breviary was ordered by John of Neumarkt in *c*.1360, while he was Bishop of Litomyšl. In addition to the usual section, it contains a history of the Holy Lance, a letter from Pope Innocent VI telling the archbishop and the bishops to announce that at the request of Charles IV he was instituting the Feast Day of the Holy Lance and Nails throughout the Empire, a spiritual portrait of St Sigismund, and the legend of St Wenceslas, as recorded by Charles IV.

particularly to the Curia in Avignon. On one such journey, he made the acquaintance of Petrarch. Ernest was also close to Charles because he was a supporter of the arts. Panel paintings and illuminated manuscripts are linked to his patronage.

John Očko of Vlašim came from the distinguished family of the lords of Jenstein and Vlašim, who held important posts at court during the reigns of John of Luxembourg and Charles IV. It is fair to assume that, like Ernest, he too attended university in Italy. From 1341 to 1352, he held the office of provost of the chapter of All Saints at Prague Castle, and was later the Bishop of Olomouc. He too was an adviser to Charles IV, who entrusted him with the education of his son Wenceslas.

After the death of Ernest, Očko – at the request of the king – became Archbishop of Prague, and two years later was conferred the title of permanent papal legate (*legatus natus*). Whenever Charles was absent from the kingdom of Bohemia for longer periods, Očko represented him in Bohemian domestic affairs. He was a man open to reform, and permitted the preaching of reform ideas in Prague, whether expressed by Conrad Waldhauser or the more radical John Milíč of Kroměříž. Očko was not without a social conscience, as was manifested in the founding of two hospitals in Prague, and, with the help of Charles IV, he founded the hospital of St Wenceslas for Bohemian pilgrims in Rome. Like his predecessor, he was a patron of the arts, not only in Prague, but also in Roudnice (Raudnitz) on the Elbe, north of Prague. He was a friend of the Augustinian monastery and, in particular, made improvements to the archbishop's castle, both of which are in Roudnice. The *Votive Panel of John Očko of Vlašim* (before 1371) was probably also intended for the castle chapel. Očko reached the zenith of his career in 1378, when, in return for his loyalty to

Pope Urban VI at the start of the Western Schism (1378–1417), he was appointed cardinal. Then – either at the request of the emperor or at the recommendation of the pope – he resigned as Archbishop of Prague, and John of Jenstein was installed in his place. As archbishop, however, Očko still celebrated a requiem for the late Charles IV, and also read a eulogy at his funeral.

Adalbert Raňkův of Ježov, was a first-rate theologian of Charles's time. His reputation as a man of learning spread far beyond the borders of the Kingdom of Bohemia. He attended the universities of Prague and Paris, where he received a doctorate in theology. For a time he worked at Paris where he taught and became a rector in 1355; he also attended Oxford. In 1369 he became a canon of St Vitus' and the *scholasticus* of the chapter (that is, its chancellor, in charge of supervising the cathedral schools). He sympathized with reform ideas, befriended John Milíč of Kroměříž, and corresponded with Conrad Waldhauser. Indeed, after he supported the lay divine Thomas of Štítný, a professor of theology at Prague labelled Raňkův a heretic. He then had to defend himself at the Curia in Avignon, and fell out of favour with Charles IV for a time. At the intercession of John of Jenstein, who was Adalbert's pupil, Charles again made his peace with Adalbert. Beginning in 1375, he again worked as a preacher in Prague. Adalbert was given the honour of holding a eulogy at the funeral of Charles IV, in which he called the deceased by the title of the emperors of ancient Rome, 'Pater patriae' (Father of the Fatherland). He bequeathed all his property to establish a scholarship for indigent students from Bohemia who wanted an education at Paris or Oxford.

A no less important figure of Charles's court was John of Neumarkt. After studying in Italy, he first worked as a parson in Silesia, and is also mentioned as a notary of the Duke of Münsterberg. He began his career at the royal court as a clerk in the chancery of King John of Bohemia, and in the reign of Charles IV he also worked as a notary. In 1353, Charles appointed him chancellor and, apart from a break in 1364–65, he retained this post for the rest of his life.

Because the appointment of a bishop contributed to the lustre of the royal chancery, Charles organized John of Neumarkt's election to the bishopric of Litomyšl. John then succeeded Očko as the Moravian metropolitan at Olomouc. He too helped to formulate the Golden Bull of 1356, and took part in important talks in the country and abroad. His work as a founder was also diverse. When, in 1374, he parted ways with Charles IV for reasons not known to us, he was forced to settle in Olomouc, the seat of his diocese. But the monarch let him remain in the post of chancellor, and did not confer it upon anyone else. Towards the end of his life John was elected Bishop of Breslau (today's Wroclaw), but died before he could take office. John was undoubtedly a co-creator of the spiritual and cultural milieu of Charles's court. The surviving catalogue of John's library provides evidence of his knowledge of thinkers of classical antiquity. He corresponded, for example, with the Roman tribune Cola di Rienzo and also with Petrarch, the latter of whom admired his abilities. As chancellor he introduced modifications based on Classical Latin to the language of chancery and diplomacy, and compiled templates for documents in Latin and German for the imperial chancery and the diocese. He also translated works into Latin and German, and wrote prayers and devotional works in an educated Latin. The scribes and illuminators whom he employed in the late 1350s created the renowned manuscript of the portable breviary called the

Paupers' Bible of Velislav

This belongs to a group of manuscripts called *Biblia Pauperum* (Paupers' Bibles), which comprise biblical stories and legends presented as a series of pictures, like an early form of the graphic novel. These manuscripts were costly and the *Velislai biblia picta*, containing 747 subtly coloured drawings, is among the largest. The manuscript was ordered by a university master and notary in Charles IV's chancery, Velislav, who is portrayed here in one of the pen-and-ink drawings. It contains the beginning of the Old Testament, part of the Gospels, the Acts of the Apostles, the Book of Revelation, and the Legend of St Wenceslas. The illustrations, by several artists, were made from 1325 to 1349. This particular example relates the story of Noah's Ark.

Liber viaticus of John of Neumarkt. Another manuscript with costly illumination is the *Missal of John of Neumarkt* (after 1364).

Also among Charles's circle of thinkers was Gall of Strahov (Havel ze Strahova). A graduate of the University of Paris, he held ecclesiastical appointments, and was an outstanding teacher of mathematics and astronomy at Prague, and was personal physician to Charles as well. He was the author of writings on hygiene, for example, about water, and emphasized the need to make gardens and wide straight streets to ensure the circulation of fresh air in the city. The streets of the New Town, whose location between Vyšehrad and the Old Town was probably influenced by Gall, were sometimes up to 29 metres wide. Gall probably also contributed to Claretus's lexicographical enterprises. Medieval men of learning appreciated Gall's astrological predictions of floods and fires in Prague. What we know about Gall of Strahov provides clear evidence that a royal physician could often enjoy the monarch's confidence and also participate in the deliberation of matters of public interest.

The Prague court of Charles IV was visited by two striking figures who left their mark in Italian history: the Roman tribune and humanist Cola di Rienzo and the Florentine poet Petrarch. Cola dreamt of the day when Rome would regain the glory it had enjoyed in the times of the Republic. With the support of the artisans, he

text within the illumination:

anno incarnacōis duice Millesimo CCxxxviii psstissimū patrem gregorīū papam nouit confirmatus est ordo fratrum Cruciferox cum stella de regula sā augustini que funda uit adhuc inseculo existens xpia uissima uirgo Agnes regali genita exprogenie patre uidelicet pziemissso il iustri rege bohemior Matre uero constancia sorore

Agnes of Bohemia, from the *Breviary of Grand Master Leo*

This illuminated manuscript, made in the milieu of a military order, is among the most beautiful Bohemian manuscripts from the reign of Charles IV. One of the illuminations shows the Blessed Agnes of Bohemia (beatified in 1874, canonized 1989) as the founder of the Knights of the Cross with the Red Star, as the Order is being placed under her protection by its first Grand Master, Albert. The Order is symbolized as a basilica. Agnes is represented here as a royal daughter, dressed in a red cloak, and wearing a royal crown. The breviary also contains remarkable illuminations of the Labours of the Months, which inspired the nineteenth-century painter Josef Mánes for his paintings of the calendar on the astronomical clock in the Old Town of Prague.

succeeded in ruling Rome for a while, but the nobles of the city came out against him, and so, in 1350, he left for the court of Charles IV in Bohemia in search of support for his ideas. He failed, however, to convince the monarch of his intentions, and Charles – in agreement with Pope Clement VI – had Cola imprisoned at the bishop's castle in Roudnice. While in Prague, Cola wrote several polemical works that influenced some of the local learned at the time. At the request of the Curia, he was taken to Avignon, where he was sentenced to death, but was ultimately released. In 1354, Pope Innocent VI sent him to Rome, so that he could help to establish papal power there. The Romans, however, considered Cola to be a usurper, and he was killed by the mob during an uprising in 1354.

Petrarch, justly called the 'Father of Humanism', in addition to his literary work, also served as a diplomat and was involved in politics. He wrote mostly in Latin, but produced some verse and essays in Italian as well. Like Cola, Petrarch longed to see a unified Italy as the heir to ancient Rome. He considered Charles IV to be a man who could make this idea a reality, and he met with him in Mantua in 1354 and in Udine in 1368, and he even visited Prague in 1356. Petrarch's correspondence with Charles IV, Archbishop Ernest of Pardubice, and the imperial chancellor John

The Emperor Charles IV, from the Gelnhausen Codex

The Codex, from the late fourteenth and the early fifteenth century, compiled by the town clerk, chief registrar, and notary in the imperial chancery, John of Gelnhausen, is essentially a set of laws in use in Jihlava (Iglau) when the town was at its zenith. Particularly noteworthy are the miniatures with splendid portraits of the kings of Bohemia, which accompany the privileges that the rulers granted to Jihlava. Charles IV is portrayed here enthroned with the emblems of his imperial rank, the coats of arms of the Empire on his right and of Bohemia on his left.

of Neumarkt from 1351 to 1368 provides evidence not only of Petrarch's ideas, but also of the penetration of proto-humanism into Bohemia.

During his time in Italy, Charles IV made the acquaintance of an apothecary called Angelo of Florence, who shortly afterwards left with Charles for Bohemia. Beginning in 1346, Angelo was employed as the court apothecary. As a gift from Charles, he received a plot of land in Jindřišská ulice (where the main post office now stands), and built a house there with a large garden (called the Hortus Angelicus) one hectare in size, where he grew medicinal herbs, vegetables, shrubs, and trees. He was so successful that in 1374 he bought house no. 144/I (called V Ráji, that is, In Paradise) at the corner of Karlova ulice and Malé náměstí (the Lesser Square), in which he probably set up a pharmacy, which was later named U Anděla (Angelo's). He bought the neighbouring house on Malé náměstí too, and also owned a vineyard where the National Museum now stands. Evidence of his high social standing is the fact that he associated with Ernest of Pardubice and John of Neumarkt, and also met Petrarch.

During the reign of Charles IV, Prague became the imperial seat, and the Bohemian Lands too reached the zenith of European culture. Whereas in the first half of the fourteenth century the country received its artistic impetuses mostly from

THEODORIC OF PRAGUE,
The Blessed Charlemagne

This is a half-figure portrait of the Blessed Charles the Great, who was in many respects a model for Charles IV. It is part of a set of 129 panel paintings decorating the Chapel of the Holy Cross at Karlstein Castle. It was most likely by Theodoric of Prague, a leading figure of medieval art in Europe. He worked at the court of Charles IV in about 1365, and, as we know from historical sources, he was the leader of the painters' Guild of St Luke in Prague. Together with the members of his workshop, he made the wall paintings and the hanging paintings of the Chapel of the Holy Cross at Karlstein. Typical features of his paintings are their monumentality, the sculpted quality of the faces, the naturalism of the details of the bodies, illusionism, and an original technique.

(50)

The Zbraslav Madonna

The *Zbraslav Madonna* (1345–50) was quite possibly donated to the Cistercian abbey in Zbraslav (the Aula Regia), just south of Prague, by Charles IV in memory of his mother Elizabeth, who was buried here. The Virgin is wearing a blue mantle with golden stars. Onto her shoulders falls her richly adorned kerchief, and she wears a royal crown, indicating that she is Queen of Heaven, and a diadem, the symbol of her virginity. The ring on the ring finger of her left hand indicates that she may also be the Bride of the Word. On her right sits the Christ Child dressed in a translucent chemise, and in His right hand He holds a goldfinch, a symbol of suffering. The golden background of the painting is decorated with stylized tendrils with leaves.

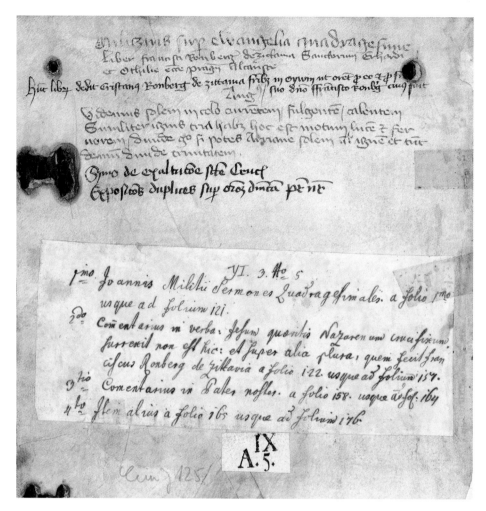

JOHN MILÍČ OF KROMĚŘÍŽ, *Sermones*
The title page of the manuscript finished in 1390.

A notary in the chancery of Charles IV, John Milíč of Kroměříž held several Church offices when, under the influence of Waldhauser's ideas, he quit all his posts in late 1363 in order to lead a life of poverty, follow Christ, and devote himself solely to preaching: at the Church of St Giles (kostel sv. Jiljí), Prague, he preached in Czech, and at the Church of St Nicholas (kostel sv. Mikuláše), also in Prague, he preached in Latin. His sermons were marked by sharp criticism of the Church and of social contradictions, and also by efforts to improve existing conditions. He was even critical of his supporter, Charles IV. Already in his own day, Milíč's sermons met with considerable response and were among those that were frequently recorded and disseminated. This influential preacher and Church reformer also founded a school of preaching, in the same house as a shelter for reformed prostitutes, which was called New Jerusalem.

abroad, particularly France and Italy, in the second half of the century figures like the architect and sculptor Peter Parler, the painters Theodoric of Prague and the Master of the Třeboň Altar were clearly contributing to the treasury of world of art with their own works. Painting and sculpture, and the decorative arts too, were exported from Bohemia to perhaps all the important countries of the Continent. The plastic arts thus became an important instrument of royal representation. Some scholars today even talk about an 'imperial style' which Charles IV made known as a distinguished patron. In the course of his reign, art experienced three styles. With John of Luxembourg new French impulses had come to Prague, as is evident

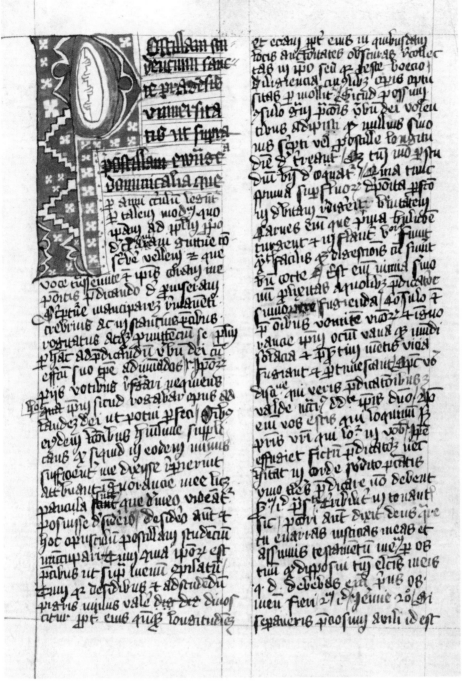

CONRAD WALDHAUSER, *Postilla studentium sanctae Pragensis universitatis*
First page of the manuscript.

An Austrian preacher and Church reformer, a forerunner of John Huss, Conrad Waldhauser came to Prague in 1362, and after a brief sojourn in the town of Litoměřice (about 64 km north-west of Prague), returned to Prague and became one of the fathers of the Bohemian reformation. For his sermons criticizing contemporary ills and urging his listeners to a life in harmony with the Gospels, he quickly became popular amongst the people of Prague, and also found favour with Charles IV. At first, he preached in the Church of St Gall and, from 1365 onwards, in the Thein Church. For his sharp criticism of simony, however, he came into conflict with some religious orders, but the pope intervened in his favour. His best-known work is the *Postilla studentium sanctae Pragensis universitatis* (Postil of the students of the holy university of Prague), which was copied in many countries of Europe.

in the sculptural decoration of the Stone Bell House on Old Town Square. Panel painting, wall painting, and book decoration were all dominated by the so-called linear style, as, for example, in the Passional of Abbess Cunigunde, the picture-book Bible known as the *Velislai biblia picta*, and the works of the Master of the Vyšší Brod Altar and his circle. The strong influence of Italy, particularly Siena, is especially evident in painting. The 'post-classic' style of French Gothic, as it moved through the Rhineland, is reflected in the workshop of the Master of the Michle Madonna. The fact that a St Eligius Guild of goldsmiths and a St Luke Guild of painters were established in Prague naturally contributed to the development of art here. Caroline art reached its zenith in the 1360s and 1370s. In 1356, Peter Parler came to Prague from Gmünd in Swabia. He introduced a dynamic, sculptural principle into architecture, which is evident in the undulating wall of the choir of St Vitus' Cathedral, the twisted composition of the staircases, and the statue of St Wenceslas in the Wenceslas Chapel there. He was involved in making the busts in the triforium and the effigies on the tombs of the dukes and kings of Bohemia in the cathedral choir. In the 1360s West European influences (from France and the Rhineland) also made their way into painting, as is evident in the works of Nicholas Wurmser of Strasbourg, to whom is attributed the Luxembourg Genealogy in the great hall of the imperial palace at Karlstein and the Relic Scenes in the Church of St Mary in the Marian Tower also at Karlstein. The greatest painter in Bohemia in this period, whose importance goes beyond the borders of the country, was doubtless Theodoric of Prague, the first artist in Bohemia to be mentioned more frequently than other painters in the records. For the Chapel of the Holy Cross at Karlstein, he and his workshop created a set of 130 panel paintings of saints (129 of which have been preserved), and he is also the painter of the wall paintings in the window reveals. Theodoric's works are characterized by great volume, plasticity of form, and naturalism, particularly evident in the details of human bodies, and his sense of space – the painting continues on to the picture frames. The shapes are modelled with shades of colour, and their transparency is also achieved with a special technique of alternating layers of tempera and oil paints. Theodoric's origins remain a mystery. His works clearly manifest Italian influences, but he was probably also trained in the Rhineland.

For Theodoric, painting the decoration of Karlstein was a unique opportunity. The original castle served as a small private seat, but Charles later gave Karlstein a special role.

After he acquired imperial relics and regalia from the heirs of Louis IV the Bavarian, in 1350, Charles decided to rebuild Karlstein and deposit the imperial crown jewels and the most holy relics in it. The two-storey palace, in which he lived, had several chapels and a great hall, covered with wall paintings with subject matter he had commissioned, including the Luxembourg Genealogy, with figures of his forebears. The most sacred room in the castle is undoubtedly the Chapel of the Holy Cross, whose decoration with panel paintings and wall paintings was carried out by Theodoric and his workshop. In this chapel were kept the imperial regalia and relics. Around the chapel runs a gilded iron rod with barbs – a symbol of the Crown of Thorns. The walls above this rod are decorated with gemstones arranged in the shape of crosses. The vaulting is covered with glass rondels and stars, the sun, and

The ceremonial entry of the Emperor of the Holy Roman Empire, Charles IV, and his son, Wenceslas IV, into Paris, from the *Grandes Chroniques de France*

In this miniature from a French chronicle written and illuminated from 1375 to 1380 is depicted the ceremonial entry of Charles IV and his son Wenceslas into Paris, to visit Charles V of France in late 1378. This state visit, which was meant to help, among other things, to resolve the Western Schism, is depicted in a number of illuminations in the manuscript. In Paris, Charles IV visited three royal seats and places linked to his youth, including the Basilica of Saint-Denis.

the moon. One enters the chapel by a staircase whose walls are decorated with the St Wenceslas and St Ludmila cycles and the ceiling with paintings of angels playing music. The reason why Charles IV had the staircase painted with these two cycles – which include a portrait of Charles and his family – is obvious: on his mother's side he belonged to the 'family of St Wenceslas'. At the very end of Charles's reign, there was again a change in the style of art, which includes distinct tendencies to make the figure seem as light as possible. The emergence of the International Style, whose outstanding proponents in Bohemia are the Master of the Třeboň Altar and the Master of the Krumlov Madonna, can reasonably be dated before 1380.

From the beginning of the 1360s onward, the first signs appeared of a crisis in the Church, caused by a decline in morals and an excessive reliance on taxation to raise revenue to cover state needs. Charles IV was aware of this situation, and at

A Reception for Charles IV, from the *Grandes Chroniques de France*

The subject of this famous miniature is a sumptuous feast held by Charles V of France in the Grand'Salle of the Palais de la Cité, Paris, in honour of the visit of the Emperor Charles IV and his son, Wenceslas IV, in 1378. From the left, in the illustration: the Bishop of Reims, the Emperor Charles IV, the King of France Charles V, the King of the Romans and of Bohemia, Wenceslas IV, and two bishops. This banquet of many courses included a re-enactment of the conquest of Jerusalem by Godfrey of Bouillon on the first crusade. During the staged battle, a magnificent ship appeared in the hall from which looked out the figure of Peter the Hermit, who may have helped to initiate the crusade.

the Imperial Diet in Mainz in 1359 he appealed to the lords spiritual to find means to put these matters right. He even threatened to confiscate the property of 'bad' priests. The pope rejected this reproach, and requested the emperor not to interfere in Church affairs. Charles supported reformist preachers, amongst whom Conrad Waldhauser and John Milíč of Kroměříž stood out. After being ordained a priest, Waldhauser became an itinerant preacher beginning in Prague in 1363, preaching at St Gall's Church and later at the Thein Church. He came out primarily against simony and the profligate lives of the clergy. But he particularly angered the Dominicans, who complained about him to Rome. The pope, however, decided in his favour. Waldhauser even became an imperial chaplain, and in November 1368 travelled to Rome to be with Charles IV, with whom he returned to Bohemia in the following year. Milíč was a reformer who was less easy to understand than Waldhauser; in one lecture he even referred to the Emperor as Antichrist.

When Urban V was elected to the Holy See, Charles IV visited him in May 1365 in Avignon (the pope's seat from 1309 to 1378). The emperor arrived at the pope's Avignon exile with great pomp, accompanied by 3,000 of his men on horseback. And he was received with no less pomp, including a great banquet held in his honour. During the visit, questions such as the matter of a crusade against the Turks and the return of the papacy to Rome were discussed. While in Provence, Charles – despite the pope's disapproval – had himself crowned King of Arles. Though Charles's efforts to have Pope Urban V returned to Rome met with success in 1367, neither the emperor nor the pope were able to assert their authority in the complicated Italian milieu, and three years later the pope decided to leave Rome again and return to Avignon. In 1373, after a two-year conflict, which threatened to erupt into war, a fortunate series of coincidences enabled the Margravate of Brandenburg to become part of the Lands of the Bohemian Crown, and it was sometimes even called 'New Bohemia'. Tangermünde Castle was rebuilt as the imperial seat. Charles's position was further buttressed by the marriage of his son Wenceslas to Joanna, a daughter of Albert I, Duke of Bavaria. In 1376, the emperor succeeded in his efforts to have the young Wenceslas IV crowned King of the Romans.

In late 1377 and early 1378, despite his worsening gout, Charles IV, accompanied by his son Wenceslas, set off for France. As he himself put it, Charles was drawn to France by the desire to see relics and pilgrimages, during which he wanted to perform devotions, and he especially wanted to meet with his nephew, Charles V of France. In addition, he intended to introduce Wenceslas, now King of the Romans and King of Bohemia, to Charles V and his other relations at the French court. One can only speculate about what the emperor wished to discuss with the king of France, but most likely it concerned current politics in Europe, including the papal Schism and the question of the successions in Poland and Hungary. The Luxembourgs were given a grand reception in Paris. Banquets and entertainments were held for them, and the emperor was given rare relics and manuscripts by Charles of France, and was also given presents by noblemen, university masters, and burghers. And the emperor also made a grand gesture – he gave the King of France the Kingdom of Arles (comprising parts of Provence and Burgundy), which had until then been imperial lands. The importance of this splendid journey is reflected in many detailed reports, concrete information, and illustrations in French chronicles from the last decades of the fourteenth century.

MASTER OF THE LUXEMBOURG GENEOLOGY (Nicholas Wurmser?), **Relic Scenes**

Charles IV was a renowned collector of relics. The wall paintings in the Church of Our Lady at Karlstein Castle, made in about 1357, depict the giving of relics to Charles IV. In the first scene, John II of France, called the Good, is making a gift of thorns from Christ's crown and a splinter from the Cross; in the middle is the donor of a now unidentifiable relic; he is either Louis I of Hungary (Louis the Great) or Peter I of Lusignan; the third scene portrays Charles IV putting the acquired relic into a golden reliquary cross.

Charles IV returned to Prague from the long and arduous journey in April 1378. The Western Schism was growing stronger, but the emperor was now too unwell to do anything about it. He died at Prague Castle, on Monday, 29 November 1378, three hours after sunset.

The remains of the emperor were embalmed and arranged so that they could be laid in state in the Royal Palace and the subjects of the Kingdom could come to pay their last respects. Attired in a purple cloak, the emperor lay on a bier covered in cloth of gold. Behind his head were three crowns: the Imperial Crown in the middle, the Iron Crown of the Lombards on the right, and the Crown of the Kings of Bohemia on the left. Other regalia, the mace, the imperial orb, and sword, were also laid out here. Eleven days later, his mortal remains were ceremoniously taken to various places in Prague: on the first day, the body lay in state at Vyšehrad overnight; on the second day, it was carried in a procession to the Church of St James (kostel sv. Jakuba) in the Old Town where it lay in state overnight; from here, the procession with the body of the late emperor crossed Charles Bridge to the Church of Our Lady under the Chain (kostel Panny Marie pod řetězem) and later, on 14 December, the procession went to Prague Castle, where his body lay in state in St Vitus' Cathedral. The funeral procession included Charles's widow, Elizabeth of Pomerania, leading noblemen and officials of the kingdom, and as many as 500 burghers dressed in black and carrying lighted candles. They were followed by the king's servants, in the same attire, and then pupils of the parish and town schools, the clergy, students, and all members of the university with the rector at their head. Behind the coffin, heralds of arms bore pennons with the coats of arms of all the lands under Charles's rule and a knight carried Charles's helmet covered in black cloth and, in his right hand, an unsheathed sword pointing downward. Behind him walked another knight, carrying the imperial military standard. The emperor's body in a purple cloak and with the imperial crown on his head rested in a simple spacious coffin under an embroidered canopy, and was borne by thirty men. It is said that as many as 7,000 people took part in the procession. In the cathedral, the emperor's body, decorated with the insignia of the Bohemian Kingdom, was laid into a pewter coffin, into which were placed the unsheathed sword, the imperial military standard, and his knight's shield. A Mass for the dead was then held. The funeral orations were given by Archbishop John Očko of Vlašim and the university master Adalbert Raňkův of Ježov, who called Charles IV 'Father of the Fatherland', a name that, in Czech history, has ever since been associated with him. At the end of this grand funeral, lasting eleven days, the signs of distinction and apparel were removed from Charles, and he was dressed in a Minorite habit. The closed coffin was placed into the tomb in the middle of St Vitus' Cathedral.

THE PRAGUE OF CHARLES IV: A GUIDE TO THE CITY

1A–C/ THE CHURCH OF SAINTS VITUS, WENCESLAS, AND ADALBERT AT PRAGUE CASTLE

In the vast precinct of Prague Castle, King John, his son and heir to the throne, Charles IV, and the Archbishop of Prague, Ernest of Pardubice, founded a cathedral on 21 November 1344. It was meant to be an expression of royal representation and to serve as a church where coronations and memorial services were held and shrines were venerated. Its construction is linked with the establishment of the archbishopric of Prague, confirmed on 30 May of that year by a papal bull. The establishment of the archiepiscopal see in Prague was vital both for Church life throughout the country and for Bohemia as an autonomous state within the empire: the king of Bohemia could now be crowned by the archbishop of Prague.

Built on the site where a rotunda had stood since the times of St Wenceslas, which was rebuilt by the later Přemyslids as a Romanesque basilica with a double choir, St Vitus' Cathedral is one of the last cathedral-type buildings in Europe. In 1344, the architect Matthew of Arras, who worked in the style that came after the classic works of the Gothic period (Chartres, Soissons, Bourges, Reims, Amiens), was invited by Charles IV to build in Prague. Matthew drew his inspiration for the apse with radiating chapels (called a chevet) from the cathedrals of Narbonne and Rodez. After Matthew's death (in 1352), the young architect Peter Parler came to Prague from the Swabian town of Gmünd in 1356. Before he died (in 1399), Parler had succeeded in building the high choir with an original net vault that visually unifies the whole space. He used this dynamic principle mainly by the wall of the cathedral choir, on the Flamboyant motifs in the pendant of the old sacristy, and in the tracery of the windows. The foundations of the nave were laid in 1392. After Parler's death, construction work was continued by the master mason Petrlík until the Hussite Wars. Nevertheless, the Cathedral of Sts Vitus, Wenceslas, and Adalbert was completed only in 1929.

1D–F/ THE GOLDEN GATE, ST VITUS' CATHEDRAL
The monumental entrance to the cathedral is among the
most valuable works of architecture of Charles IV's Prague.
According to the chronicle of Benedict Krabice of Weitmühle
the tripartite portal was finished in 1367, the mosaic in
1370–71. It was probably executed by Venetian mosaicists
and their Bohemian apprentices, perhaps on a design by
the painter Niccolò (Nicoletto) Semitecolo. It is called the
Golden Gate because the background of the mosaic is gilded
and, according to contemporary testimony, in the right light
it glowed golden. Its centre is dominated by Christ in a
mandorla surrounded by angels with the Instruments of the
Passion. On the left-hand side of the mandorla the Virgin
and a group of six Apostles kneel on a cloud; on the right
are St John the Baptist and the other six Apostles. Below
the mandorla, Christ is being worshipped by six patron
saints of Bohemia, who are kneeling: Wenceslas, Adalbert,
Vitus, Ludmila, Sigismund, and Procopius. Below them,
on the sides at the top of the middle arch kneel Charles IV
and Elizabeth of Pomerania. In the first register on the lower
left (on Christ's right), an angel helps the Blessed to rise from
the grave and shows them the way to heaven. In the lower
right-hand register, the Archangel Michael drives the Damned
to hell.

2/ THE CHOIR OF ST VITUS' CATHEDRAL

The medieval choir of the cathedral was built from 1344 to 1420. The first architect of the cathedral, Matthew of Arras, built the choir chapels and the foundations of the old sacristy. On them, Peter Parler built the choir in 1356. His lodge built the high choir with the triforium and covered it with net vaulting. The Parler lodge also carried out a remarkable vault with pendants in the old sacristy, and built the chapels of St Wenceslas and St Sigismund as well as much of the cathedral tower. The Parler lodge introduced some dynamic elements into the architecture of the choir, which are particularly evident in the visual undulation of the choir walls, which disrupts the typical vertical order of late High Gothic architecture.

FROM THE TREASURY OF ST VITUS'

A GOLDEN RELIQUARY CROSS OF THE KINGDOM OF BOHEMIA (obverse & reverse)
This cross, imprecisely called a coronation cross, is, together with the royal crown, among the most precious pieces of goldsmith's work in the St Vitus' Treasury. The base of the cross is from the thirteenth century, and was modified in about 1357; the foot is later. The cross, made of pure gold and almost a metre high, is of the Greek type. It is decorated with an emerald, sapphires, spinals, and Roman and Byzantine cameos. Concealed in the cross are rare relics connected mainly with Christ, the Virgin, Sts Anne, John the Baptist, John the Evangelist, and Pancras. The obverse of the cross is set with relics of the True Cross – two crossed pieces of cedar; on the reverse are two thorns from the Crown of Thorns, part of a Nail, part of the Holy Sponge, which was dipped in vinegar (or posca) and offered to Christ to drink on the Cross, and part of the rope which He was bound with when flogged. Originally, the cross was kept at Karlstein Castle.

ONYX CHALICE OF CHARLES IV

This remarkable Communion chalice from the Treasury of
St Vitus' is made from a single piece of translucent, golden
brown (and in places reddish) onyx, in which opaque white
tracery-like patterns meander to form the ornamentation.
The chalice, 7 cm deep, is decorated with silver-gilt mounts
including four vertical bands imprinted with tiny rosettes,
and attached to an ellipsoid foot decorated with the coats
of arms of the King of the Romans (that is, King of the
Germans) and the King of Bohemia: two of the shields bear
the Bohemian lion, the other two the Imperial eagle. From
the inscription on the gilded foot, it is clear that the chalice
was commissioned by Charles IV in 1350, which was declared
a Holy Year (a Jubilee). From the records it is also clear that
the chalice was used in the Communion of the Sick. It was
made by Prague goldsmiths, who were among some of the
best in Europe at that time.

A GOTHIC RELIQUARY OF THE PARLER TYPE
(obverse & reverse)

St Vitus' Treasury also contains a tower-shaped reliquary, whose four-lobed foot bears the blue and red enamelled emblem of the Parler family, the master masons of St Vitus' Cathedral. The reliquary has a rock crystal compartment containing relics of St Benedict. On the reverse is a sculptural relief of the Host. There is good reason to believe that it was made by the Parler workshop, because amongst the forms used on the reliquary is Flamboyant tracery, typical of their work. The reliquary is first mentioned in the St Vitus' Treasury inventory in 1420. It was probably made *c.*1400 to commemorate Peter Parler, who died in 1399.

A VERA ICON OF ST VITUS' CATHEDRAL

The Treasury of St Vitus' includes three *vera icons* (true images or Holy Faces of Christ). Charles IV brought the first copy of the devotional image from Rome to Prague probably as early as 1355. There is even a legend that he brought the original painting to Bohemia and left a mere copy in the Basilica of St Peter. The earliest *vera icon* in the St Vitus' Treasury is painted on paper (or perhaps parchment) and affixed to a later wooden panel in a Baroque frame. It probably served as the model for the second *vera icon* (from 1370–80), which is painted in brown on whitish grey parchment glued to a walnut panel. The background of the painting is covered with gold leaf, hence the Golden Vera Icon. The earliest copy, from between 1400 and 1410, is set in a painted frame decorated with figures of angels and the six patron saints of Bohemia. Apart from the version of the Veil of St Veronica, we also know about the making of the *vera icon*, as a picture 'not made by human hands' (an *acheiropoietos*), from the Legend of Abgar, where it is called the Mandylion. According to one version of the legend, Abgar, King of Edessa, was ill and sent for his painter Hannan to make a portrait of the Saviour's face, which was supposed to cure the king. The painter, however, did not succeed in making the portrait. Consequently, Jesus took the tablecloth and imprinted it with his own image, and this is what the painter brought back to the king. The king put this cloth onto his own face and was cured.

4/ THE TOMB OF OTTOKAR I PŘEMYSL, THE ROYAL BURIAL PLACE, ST VITUS' CATHEDRAL

Emulating the Basilica of Saint-Denis, Paris, which became the burial place of the kings of France and their families, Charles IV had the tombs of his forebears – the Přemyslid dukes and kings – built in the choir chapels of St Vitus' Cathedral. The Imperial Chapel contains the tombs of the dukes Bretislaus I and Spytihněv II. The Chapel of St Antony Abbot holds the tomb of the dukes Bretislaus II and Bořivoj II. The Saxon Chapel contains the tombs of the kings Ottokar I Přemysl and Ottokar II Přemysl. The weekly accounts of the cathedral lodge show that the tomb of Ottokar I Přemysl, which bears his effigy, was carved by Peter Parler in 1377.

(77)

5/ A CORBEL IN ST VITUS' CATHEDRAL

This corbel, carved with the figures of Adam and Eve, is in the chevet of the choir. The work of the Parler lodge, it was probably intended for a statue of the Virgin, the 'New Eve', redeeming the sin of the Old Testament Eve; Christ, as the 'New Adam', absolved the old Adam's sin.

6A–H/ PORTRAITS ON THE TRIFORIUM, ST VITUS' CATHEDRAL

The inner and the outer triforium of St Vitus' Cathedral are decorated with figurative and ornamental sculpture. The inner (lower) triforium has 21 busts made by sculptors from the Parler lodge. This portrait gallery may usefully be divided into three groups according to date of origin. Between 1375 and 1380, three stylized masks were made, as were the scene of a dog and cat fighting and the busts of the members of the imperial family: John Henry, Blanche of Valois, Anne of Bavaria, Anne of Schweidnitz, Elizabeth of Pomerania, Charles IV, John of Luxembourg, Elizabeth of Bohemia, Wenceslas IV, and Johanna of Bavaria. The second group comprises busts carved after 1380: Wenceslas of Luxembourg (of Bohemia), Benedict Krabice of Weitmühle, Ondřej Kotlík, Matthew of Arras, Peter Parler, Ernest of Pardubice, John Očko of Vlašim, John of Jenstein, Mikuláš Holubec, and Leonard Bušek. The latest, after 1385, is the bust of Wenceslas of Radetz (Václav z Radče).

On the outer (upper) triforium, next to the decorative sculptures with subject matter related to the life and manners of the time, are busts of Christ, the Virgin, and the Bohemian patron saints Wenceslas, Ludmila, Procopius, Adalbert, Vitus, Sigismund of Burgundy, and Cyril and Methodius. All the busts were made by the Parler lodge from 1372 to 1380. The location of the bust of the Emperor Charles IV on the lower triforium corresponds to that of Christ on the upper triforium, suggesting that Charles considered himself Christ's representative on earth.

6A/ JOHN OF LUXEMBOURG

The father of Charles IV, John of Luxembourg, was the son of
Henry VII, Count of Luxembourg and King of the Romans,
and Margaret of Brabant, the niece of Philip IV of France, who
was called the Fair. Born in 1296, John grew up at Philip's court.
In 1310 he married Elizabeth (Eliška Přemyslovna), four years
his senior. A year later, he was crowned King of Bohemia. The
new ruler was soon disappointed with circumstances in the
kingdom, for it was run by the nobility. He spent little time
in Bohemia, which led to social breakdown in the country.
He achieved greater success in foreign policy, acquiring the
Egerland (Chebsko, in Czech) for the Kingdom of Bohemia
as a fiefdom, followed by Upper Lusatia and, later, in 1335,
a large part of Silesia. In 1331, the Emperor Louis IV made
John liege lord of the north Italian towns of Bergamo, Bobbio,
Brescia, Cremona, Milan, Novara, and Pavia, and King John
then inherited Lucca. He loved tournaments and was seriously
wounded in one in 1321. His secretary and diplomat of
many years was the distinguished French poet and composer
Guillaume de Machaut. In 1339, John went blind, yet in 1346 he
fought in the Battle of Crécy, in which he died a hero's death,
and soon became known as the 'dernier des rois chevaliers'
(last of the knight-kings).

6B/ ELIZABETH OF BOHEMIA
(ELIŠKA PŘEMYSLOVNA)

The mother of Charles IV, Elizabeth was a Přemyslid. She was one of the ten children of Wenceslas II, the King of Bohemia and of Poland, and Judith of Habsburg. She received a thorough education at the Convent of St George at Prague Castle from her aunt, Cunigunde of Bohemia (Kunhuta Přemyslovna), the Abbess there. After the murder of Wenceslas III, the last male member of the house of Přemyslid, a struggle for the throne arose between Henry of Bohemia (Heinrich von Kärnten) and Rudolph of Habsburg (Rudolf I of Bohemia). Discontented nobles united with the abbots of the great Cistercian houses and with his father, the Emperor Henry VII, successfully negotiated the marriage of Princess Elizabeth and John of Luxembourg. Several children were born of this not very happy union, of whom the Emperor and King Charles IV and his brother John Henry, later the Margrave of Moravia, achieved the greatest renown. In 1319 the marriage of Elizabeth and John finally broke down. Elizabeth was the last member of the Přemyslid line. Towards the end of her life, she collected relics, supported religious houses, and tried to have Agnes of Bohemia canonized. She died at the age of 38, and was buried in the Cistercian abbey (called the Aula regia in Latin and Königsaal in German) at Zbraslav (now a southern suburb of Prague).

6C/ CHARLES IV

The bust of the Emperor Charles IV on the triforium of
St Vitus' Cathedral occupies the place of honour directly on
the axis of the choir. In its placement it corresponds to the
bust of Christ on the outer part of the triforium, thereby
suggesting that the monarch is Christ's representative on
earth. Opposite the emperor's bust is the bust of his last
wife, Elizabeth of Pomerania. Next to him are the busts
of Charles's other three wives, his son Wenceslas IV, and
his son's first wife, Joanna of Bavaria. Then come Charles's
parents, brothers, the archbishops of Prague, and the clerks
of the works. It is remarkable that the busts of the master
masons (architects) of the cathedral, Matthew of Arras
and Peter Parler, also appear in this august company.

6D/ BLANCHE OF VALOIS

The first and most beloved wife of King Charles IV, Blanche of Valois was born to Charles, Count of Valois, and his third wife, Mahaut of Châtillon. She was brought up at the court of the King of France, her cousin, Charles the Fair, and his wife Mary, the younger sister of John of Luxembourg. On 15 May 1323, still a child, Blanche, with the agreement of Pope John XXII, was married to Charles IV. Eleven years later, she travelled to Prague to be with her husband. A year later, she give birth to a daughter, Margaret (the future Queen of Hungary), and, in 1342, to another daughter, Catherine (the future Electress Consort of Brandenburg). In September 1347 Blanche was crowned Queen of Bohemia, but the following year, after a short illness, she died. She is the only one of Charles's four wives to be portrayed in the triforium with plaited hair. In the now Polish town of Środa Śląska (Neumarkt, in German) a hoard called the Środa Treasure was discovered in the late 1980s, which included a splendid crown, probably belonging to Blanche. It was among the various items that Charles IV may have pawned to local Jews.

6E/ ANNE OF BAVARIA
(ANNE OF THE PALATINATE)

Charles's second wife, Anne of Bavaria was the daughter
of Rudolph II, Count Palatine of the Rhine, and Anne of
Bavaria, whose great-uncle, Henry, Duke of Carinthia, had
been King of Bohemia. It was a political marriage: Anne's
father supported the anti-king Günther von Schwarzburg,
and Charles, by marrying Anne, eliminated this support. The
marriage took place in 1349, and that same year Anne was
crowned Queen of the Romans and of Bohemia. She gave
birth to a son, Wenceslas, but he died soon after being born.
Queen Anne died on 2 February 1353, when she fell from her
horse and broke her neck.

6F/ ANNE OF SCHWEIDNITZ

In 1352, at the age of 37, Charles married for a third time. His new bride was the fourteen-year-old Anne of Schweidnitz (Świdnica), the daughter of Henry II, Duke of Schweidnitz, and Catherine of Hungary. Anne was brought up at the Hungarian royal court. Originally, Charles IV intended to marry Anne to his son Wenceslas, but when the boy died at the age of two, Charles married her himself. In addition to a young bride, Charles thus also gained control of the Piast Duchies of Silesia, since Anne was the heiress of her uncle, Bolko II, Duke of Opole. In 1353, she was crowned Queen of Bohemia and, a year later, Queen of the Romans. In Rome, in 1355, she was crowned Empress. In 1358, her daughter Elizabeth was born, and, three years later, at the imperial castle in Nuremberg, she gave birth to the heir Charles had long hoped for, Wenceslas IV. Anna died in 1362, after giving birth to a third child.

6G/ ELIZABETH OF POMERANIA

The daughter of Bogislaw V, Duke of Pomerania, and his
wife, Elizabeth of Poland (the daughter of Casimir III, King
of Poland, called the Great), Elizabeth became Charles's
fourth wife, in 1363. This marriage too was politically
motivated, for in this way Charles IV undermined the unity
of the anti-Luxembourg coalition, of which Elizabeth's
father was an important member. Their grand wedding took
place in Cracow. A month later, she was crowned Queen of
Bohemia, and, in 1368, Empress of the Holy Roman Empire.
She became famous for her physical strength: according
to the chronicles, she broke swords and horseshoes. Theirs
was a harmonious marriage, and she gave birth to six
children: Anne (1366–94; Queen of England), Sigismund
(1368–1437; King of Hungary, Holy Roman Emperor, King
of Bohemia), John (1370–96; Duke of Görlitz and Margrave
of Brandenburg), Charles (1372–73), Margaret (1373–1410;
Burgravine of Nuremberg), and Henry (1377–78).

6H/ WENCELSAS IV

The son of Charles IV and Anne of Schweidnitz, Wenceslas was heir to the Bohemian throne. He was made king at the age of two, and Charles IV, in 1376, helped him to acquire the crown of the King of the Romans. His tutors were Ernest of Pardubice and then John Očko of Vlašim. In 1370, he married Joanna of Bavaria, and in 1389, Sophia of Bavaria. Neither marriage, however, resulted in children. Wenceslas IV was an educated man; he owned a large library with magnificent illuminated manuscripts. At first he supported the reform movement in the Church and supported John Huss (Jan Hus) and Prague University. He also completed several of the building works begun by his father. After the death of Charles IV, Wenceslas proved himself less able to perform his duties as monarch, and came into conflict with the archbishop, the nobles, and his own relations. He had the support only of his half-brother, John of Görlitz. He was even twice imprisoned by rebellious noblemen, and in 1400 was deposed from the imperial throne. He died in 1419, on the eve of the Hussite Wars. He was initially buried in the abbey church at Zbraslav, but his remains were later translated to St Vitus' Cathedral.

7/ A CAT AND A DOG FIGHTING

On the lower triforium of the Cathedral the Parler lodge
carved not only the busts of the imperial family, the
archbishops, and the clerks of works and architects of the
cathedral, but also several decoratively symbolic subjects.
Among the most remarkable is a relief depicting a cat and
a dog fighting. This is probably a symbolic expression of the
struggle between light and darkness.

8/ ST WENCESLAS

The bust of St Wenceslas on the outer part of the triforium of St Vitus' Cathedral is part of a set of sculptures representing the Heavenly Jerusalem. The original appearance of the bust has been considerably damaged by weathering and also subsequent restoration.

The ideological centre of St Vitus' Cathedral is the Chapel
of St Wenceslas. It was built by the Parler lodge on a square
plan and covered with a net vault. It was consecrated on the
Feast Day of St Wenceslas, 1367, a year after it was finished.
Charles IV had a splendid tomb built here for the principal
Bohemian patron saint. It was decorated in gold reliefs
with the figures of St Wenceslas, Charles IV himself, and
Elizabeth of Pomerania, as well as the martyrdoms of the
Bohemian patron saints and the Apostles. On a little
pedestal of the tomb stood a golden bust incorporating the
skull of St Wenceslas, on which was placed the Bohemian
crown. The walls of the chapel were encrusted with gemstones
and decorated with wall paintings of the Passion and Glory of
Christ. The main altar in the chapel was dedicated to St John
the Evangelist. The wall paintings with the St Wenceslas cycle
date from the beginning of the sixteenth century.

TABERNACLE OF THE WENCESLAS CHAPEL

In the right-hand corner of the altar wall of the St Wenceslas
Chapel stands a metal tabernacle, the receptacle for the
Host. It is the work of a lodge blacksmith called Wenceslas,
from 1375. The tabernacle is in the form of a tower ornately
decorated in the style of the Gothic architecture of Peter
Parler and with the coats of arms of Bohemia and the Empire
on the corner buttresses. It was originally located on a raised
pedestal with steps. This tabernacle may reflect the intended
final appearance of the Great Tower of St Vitus' Cathedral.

GEM-ENCRUSTED WALLS OF THE WENCESLAS CHAPEL

The gemstone decoration of the walls of the St Wenceslas Chapel
was probably completed in 1366 at the same time as the chapel.
The cut and polished gems come from Ciboušov, north Bohemia.
A band of the wall, 150 cm in height, is covered with 1,484 tablets
of amethyst, jasper, chrysoprase, topaz, agate, and citrine, all set
into the mortar. The incrustation is made even more precious
by the gilded surface of the stucco.

Considering that the chapel has a square plan and is consecrated
not only to St Wenceslas but also to St John the Evangelist, to
whom authorship of the Book of Revelation is sometimes attributed,
it is very likely that the gemstones decoration of the walls refers to
the idea of the Heavenly Jerusalem, whose walls are described as
being made of gemstones. Similarly, the walls of the Chapel of the
Holy Cross at Karlstein (consecrated in 1365) and of the Chapel of
St John the Evangelist at Tangermünde Castle (completed in 1374),
also one of Charles's imperial seats, were similarly decorated.

After a visit to the chapel, the French writer Guillaume Apollinaire
wrote the poem 'Zone' (1913), which includes the lines 'Horrified
you see your own features drawn in the agates of St Vitus'. / You
were so sad you could have died the day you saw yourself there.'

Flagellation of Christ.

CORBELS IN THE WENCESLAS CHAPEL

The north entrance to the Chapel of St Wenceslas has two corbels. The first bears a figure of St Peter, the second figure is of the Devil ripping out Judas' tongue. Two paths are depicted here: the first, of piety, leading to salvation, the second, the path of betrayal and sin, leading to damnation. The west entrance to the chapel was decorated with a *vera icon* (Holy Face), which usually has an apotropaic function when placed above an entrance (that is, it was meant to ward off evil).

10/ STATUE OF ST WENCESLAS, THE ST WENCESLAS CHAPEL

Who made the statue of St Wenceslas remains a question. In the weekly accounts of the St Vitus' Cathedral lodge it is stated that in 1373 the mason Heinrich Parler worked for five days on a statue, but that would not be long enough to have completed this one. It seems most likely that he actually only finished the work of Peter Parler, since the pedestal bears the mason's marks of Peter Parler. From the accounts of the cathedral lodge, we may deduce that the statue was probably polychromed by the court painter Oswald. The original location of the statue is also unclear. Was it initially intended for the exterior of the Wenceslas Chapel, where there is a stone canopy, or for its interior? There is strong evidence that it was in the chapel interior from the 1480s onward, as is attested to by the figures of angels and the Bohemian patron saints on the altar wall of the chapel.

11/ THE BAPTISM OF ST ODILIA, VLAŠIM CHAPEL

The Vlašim Chapel (also called the Chapel of Sts Erhard and Odilia) is decorated with a large set of wall paintings. At his own expense, Archbishop John Očko of Vlašim had an altar built here in 1367 and dedicated it to Sts Erhard and Odilia, at which time the chapel was also decorated with the wall paintings. On the east wall is a monumentally conceived scene of the Baptism of St Odilia, the patroness of people afflicted with blindness or eye disease, and to whom Očko prayed for intercession, because he suffered from a serious eye affliction. Another of the paintings portrays Očko venerating the Man of Sorrows (holding the Cross), Adalbert, the patron saint of the archdiocese, and Catherine, the patron saint of learning, especially philosophy. After his death, Očko was buried in this chapel under a tombstone with his effigy carved by the Parler lodge.

12/ ADORATION OF THE MAGI, SAXON CHAPEL

This wall painting in the Saxon Chapel (also known as the Chapel of St Adalbert, St Dorothy, and the Relics) is simply magnificent. This chapel, in the south-east part of the choir, was probably built during the first stage of the construction work. It was acquired at some unknown date by Rudolph I, Duke of Saxe-Wittenberg (and Elector of Saxony), who used to stay at Charles's court. The technique used in the wall painting is tempera with an oil-based binder, painted onto the smoothed ashlars of the wall. In its composition, the painting follows on from the *Adoration of the Magi* by Theodoric of Prague, in the Chapel of the Holy Cross at Karlstein. It is different from that work in its greater sense of space and also in making the figures appear as materially light as possible, which is particularly evident in the delicate figure of the Virgin. One of the portrayed Magi has the features of the Emperor Charles IV. The painter was obviously acquainted with the progressive trends of the Franco-Flemish area, and he was probably the one who most thoroughly showed the way to the new style known today as International Gothic.

13/ THE CHURCH OF ALL SAINTS

While still only Margrave of Moravia, Charles IV founded a special chapter of canons, in 1341, at the palace Chapel of All Saints. Built in the Romanesque style at the Castle precinct in the twelfth century, the chapel was later remodelled and enlarged. In 1366, it was incorporated into the Collegium Carolinum (today's Karolinum): members of the chapter at All Saints' were mostly masters at Prague University. Charles decided to build a new chapel for the chapter, for which his inspiration was the Sainte-Chapelle, Paris. From 1370 to 1387, on a design by Peter Parler, the Parler lodge erected a narrow single-aisled building with three bays of vaulting and a chevet (apse) comprising seven sides of a dodecagon. The building was badly damaged by the great fire that swept through the Castle in 1541, and the chapel had to be rebuilt.

14/ THE PALACE OF CHARLES IV, PRAGUE CASTLE

In his autobiography, *Vita Caroli*, Charles IV writes that when he arrived in Prague he found the Castle damaged right down to the foundations after a fire in 1303. Upon his arrival in Bohemia in 1333, while still Margrave of Moravia, he began construction work on a new building, which was modelled on the French royal palace. The main room, remarked Charles, was a 'large and lovely hall'. It ceased to exist after the Jagiellon remodelling of the palace in the late fifteenth century. Of the original palace, only several vaulted rooms on the lower floors have been preserved.

15/ BISHOP'S COURT (BISKUPSKÝ DVŮR)

The seat of the bishop and archbishop of Prague was in the Lesser Town. It occupied the area delimited by the streets Mostecká, Josefská, and Letenská, and Dražické náměstí (Dražice Square). In the 1170s, the bishops built a little castle here for themselves so that they would be less dependent on the temporal powers than they had been when they settled at Prague Castle. Bishop's Court is first mentioned in the records in 1249. We may deduce its appearance only from the written records, because it was destroyed during the Hussite Wars. All that remains is the tower with the emblem of Bishop John IV of Dražice, an arched upright branch of vine with three leaves.

16A,B/ THE CHURCH OF ST MARY UNDER THE CHAIN (PANNY MARIE POD ŘETĚZEM)

Soon after their arrival in the Lesser Town of Prague, the Knights Hospitallers acquired an advantageous site by the river, upon which they began to build a Romanesque basilica with a nave flanked by an aisle on each side, which was completed before 1182. It was remodelled in the Gothic style probably after 1314, when the Hospitallers acquired the property of the Knights Templar, after the latter Order was dissolved by Pope Clement V in 1312. The presbytery of the church was for the most part probably ready in 1378, and the body of the late Emperor and King, Charles IV, lay in state there. By the outbreak of the Hussite Wars, the porch flanked by robust towers was completed, and the gable and the foundations of the piers of the arcades of the left aisle were also finished. In 1420, the Hussites set fire to the commandery. After another fire, in the early sixteenth century, the choir was given new vaulting. All that remains of the medieval art in the presbytery is a fragment of a painting of the Man of Sorrows (showing a seated Christ) and a Late Gothic Madonna.

17/ THE HUNGER WALL (HLADOVÁ ZEĎ)

The Hunger Wall, sometimes also called the Toothed Wall (Zubatá zeď), was ordered built from 1360 to 1362 by the emperor and king, Charles IV, as part of the fortifications of the Lesser Town, which was meant to make difficult an attack on Prague from the south or the west. Between 4 and 4.5 metres in height and 1.8 metres in width, it was built of marlstone (impure argillaceous limestone) blocks on the slopes of Petřín Hill (formerly Lawrence Hill). It wound its way from Újezd (now a part of the Lesser Town) over Strahov Hill to Hradčany (the district around Prague Castle). The upper part of the walls had embrasures, battlements, and walkways. The fortification also included several bastions. The legend behind the names Hunger Wall and Toothed Wall is flattering to the emperor: he allegedly had it built so that the poor of Prague could earn enough money to feed themselves or at least to buy something to nibble on. The walls have been repaired several times over the centuries.

18/ CHARLES BRIDGE

On 1 February 1342, a flood destroyed the Romanesque bridge
that had been built by Princess Judith, the wife of Vladislav II.
Consequently, on 9 July 1357, Charles IV ceremonially
laid the foundation stone of the new bridge. According to
the inscription under his bust on the triforium of St Vitus'
Cathedral, Peter Parler was also in charge of the building of
the bridge. His inspiration may have been the Roman Bridge
in Trier or the bridge of fourteen arches over the River Moselle
at Braubach, just south-east of Koblenz, which was built by
Charles's great uncle, Baldwin of Luxembourg, Archbishop-
Elector of Trier. The bridge over the Vltava, with sixteen
arches, spanning a total length of 516 metres, and with a width
of 9.5 metres, must have been basically ready by 1378, because
Charles IV's funeral procession crossed it. But it was not truly
finished until the beginning of the fifteenth century. The bridge
has a tower both on its Lesser Town and on its Old Town end.

19A–E/ THE BRIDGE TOWER ON THE OLD TOWN SIDE (STAROMĚSTSKÁ MOSTECKÁ VĚŽ)

Erected in honour of Charles IV and his son Wenceslas IV, the tower is essentially a triumphal arch. It was built in the 1370s and 1380s by Peter Parler and his lodge as part of the fortifications of Charles Bridge. The decoration of the tower façades is particularly remarkable, and Charles IV undoubtedly participated in the conception of its symbolism. The façade from the Old Town side is divided by cornices into three stages. On the uppermost stage, set into frames of the architecture, are the figures of two Bohemian patron saints: Procopius (or perhaps Adalbert) and Sigismund. Just below them is a heraldic lion. In the second register, architecturally bordered as if to depict a church in cross section, is the figure of St Vitus floating above two arches of a miniature bridge. Enthroned on his right is the Emperor Charles IV, with his son Wenceslas IV on Vitus' left. They are accompanied, from left to right, by the coats of arms of Prague, the empire, Bohemia, and Moravia, and, at the top of the church cross section, the coat of arms of St Wenceslas.

The kingfishers in torses (heraldic wreaths of twisted fabric) are symbols of the court of Wenceslas IV. On the lowest stage of the tower is a 'gallery' of coats of arms of the Lands of the Bohemian Crown and another pair of kingfishers in torses. The figurative corbels and the corbels with fighting animals are also remarkable. The bay of net vaulting in the tower gate is decorated with figures of women bath-attendants and kingfishers in torses. The side facing Prague Castle was also decorated with sculpture. It is generally assumed to have included a figure of the Virgin enthroned with Sts Wenceslas and Adalbert, but was destroyed by the Swedes in the siege of the Old Town in 1648, towards the end of the Thirty Years' War. The staircase inside the tower terminates with a remarkable sculpture of a tower keeper.

20A,B/ THE OLD TOWN TOWN HALL
(STAROMĚSTSKÁ RADNICE)

The east wing of the town hall of the Old Town is dominated
by a tower from the 1360s. The corner is decorated with a
stone statue of the Madonna, a remarkable example in the
development of such statues, made in 1356–57 by an artist
very familiar with French sculpture. (The original is in the
City of Prague Museum.) It may well be an early work of the
Parler lodge. In 1381 the town hall chapel was consecrated
to patron saints of the Bohemian Lands – Wenceslas, Vitus,
Adalbert, Ludmila, Procopius, and Sigismund – statues of
whom stood on corbels under stone canopies between the
windows. The façade of this wing is decorated with a 'gallery'
of coats of arms: below the crown cornice are the arms of
the Empire, the historic Lands of the Bohemian Crown, the
Old Town, and the Archbishopric of Prague; below them are
emblems of town councillors from about 1360.

21A–D/ THE THEIN CHURCH
(KOSTEL MATKY BOŽÍ PŘED TÝNEM)

The main church of the Old Town, also known as the Church
of the Virgin before the Thein (kostel Panny Marie před
Týnem or simply the Týnský chrám), has dominated Old
Town Square since the Middle Ages. Construction work on
this church began on the site of a Romanesque church in
the third quarter of the fourteenth century. In about 1380,
the choir and both choir chapels were completed. The sedile
with busts of a king (perhaps Charles IV) and a queen in the
south choir chapel probably dates from the end of Charles's
reign. It was most likely in the 1360s that the decoration
of the north portal began. The apse has a pier in the main
axis of the choir, a frequent feature of fourteenth-century
Bohemian architecture.

As is clear from the Imperial and the Bohemian coats of arms there, the north portal of the Thein Church was meant to represent the temporal powers. The portal was installed late in the reign of Charles IV and was finished in the reign of his son, Wenceslas IV. The tympanum of the portal is decorated with expressively executed scenes of the Passion. Originally, the archivolt of the portal probably had statues of the twelve Apostles and the four Evangelists. The corbels, decorated with subject matter referring to the relationship between the Old and the New Testament, the Resurrection, and the Eucharist, most probably supported statutes of the Man of Sorrows and the Virgin of Mercy. The sculptural decoration of the north portal is partly the work of the Parler lodge at St Vitus'.

22A–E/ STONE BELL HOUSE (DŮM U KAMENNÉHO ZVONU)

The house on the corner of Staroměstké náměstí and Týnská ulice was part of the residence of the recently wed John of Luxembourg and Elizabeth of Bohemia, after their arrival in Prague in 1310. The house is named after the stone bell on its corner. The bell may commemorate John's arrival in Prague to depose Henry, King of Bohemia (*reg.* 1306 and 1307–10, and Duke of Carinthia), when local Luxembourg supporters, as agreed in advance, would ring the bell of the Thein Church as a signal to attack the guarded gate. The façade of what appears to have been a grand burgher's house was decorated with enthroned figures of the king and queen, accompanied by heraldic supporters; on the upper storey there were probably figures of the patron saints of Bohemia. The house had two chapels, both decorated with wall paintings from *c.*1340. The Stone Bell House is a possible birthplace of Charles IV's.

The Killing of St Wenceslas – detail, west wall of the chapel.

The Killing of St Wenceslas – detail with animal symbols, west wall of the chapel.

Man of Sorrow and the Instruments of the Passion (Arma Christi) – the altar wall.

Figure of a female saint – north wall of the chapel.

23A–F/ ROTLEV HOUSE, THE CAROLINUM

The original house, which became the core of the Carolinum, was built by the master of the royal mint, Johlin Rotlev, a member of a rich Prague family. Sometime in 1375–76 he bequeathed the finished building to his son, Martin, who sold it to King Wenceslas IV in 1385. A year later Wenceslas sold the remodelled house to Charles University. Despite its radical nineteenth-century Revivalist alterations (carried out from 1879 to 1881), the chapel with the oriel is the most artistically striking part of the medieval Carolinum. Its Gothic exterior is covered in ornate architectural ornamentation, sculptures, and heraldic emblems. It is generally assumed that statues of patron saints of the Bohemian Lands – Wenceslas, Ludmila, Adalbert, Vitus, Procopius, and Sigismund – were originally placed below the six stone canopies. In the panels below the chapel windows are the emblems of the King of Bohemia (the lion), Elizabeth of Pomerania (the griffin), Margrave John Henry (or perhaps Jobst) of Moravia (the eagle), Archbishop John Očko of Vlašim (or perhaps John of Jenstein) (the vultures' heads), and the Rotlev family (Rotlöwe; the red lion on steps). The architectural sculpture (people, fighting animals, and green men,) shows the influence of the Parler lodge at St Vitus' Cathedral.

The oblong interior space of the Rotlev house, covered with four bays of groin vaults and originally open towards Ovocný trh (the Fruit Market), resembles a cloister. It was built from 1370 to 1380. It was from here that one entered a room called the *fiscus*, which served as the university treasury and archive. Attached to it was a vaulted room, today called the Imperial Hall, and a jail for student offenders.

In about 1360 a window was made from the covered walk of Rotlev House to the *mázhaus* (*Maßhaus*, in German; a room that served commercial purposes). The stone mullion and transom form a cross in the window. Considering the other exacting work that went into the construction of this grand house, it is reasonable to assume that the window was glazed with glass roundels.

24/ THE CHURCH OF THE HOLY SPIRIT (KOSTEL SV. DUCHA)

This church is located right beside what used to be the Jewish ghetto. Next to the church a Benedictine provostry was built, but ceased to exist during the Hussite Wars. The church is a fairly simple aisleless structure from the second quarter of the fourteenth century, whose medieval character was wiped away by Baroque remodelling. The church contains a much venerated *Pietà* (1410–20) attributed to the Master of the Týn Calvary.

(135)

25/ THE CHURCH OF ST CASTULUS (KOSTEL SV. HAŠTALA)

The church, comprising a basilica with a nave, two aisles, and a polygonal apse, stands on the site of an earlier Romanesque sanctuary. Work on the new Gothic building began *c.*1310, and by the mid-fourteenth century the church had a polygonal apse and three bays of vaulting over the nave and the south aisle. The nave, the north aisle, and the west façade were probably completed by 1375. The north aisle is like a two-aisled hall, and the forms used reflect the advanced state of architecture built in the reign of Wenceslas IV. It was undoubtedly erected with the participation of masons from the Parler cathedral lodge in Prague, as is attested by the masterfully executed corbels from which the ribs spring. In the east, the sacristy with the treasury above it is attached to the choir and connected directly to the double-aisled hall. It seems that the sacristy was originally the Chapel of All Saints, which was founded and funded by Pešek of Příboj and Litovice in 1375. Fragments of wall paintings from several periods have been discovered inside. From the third quarter of the fourteenth century come the wall paintings with the Genealogy of Christ, half-figures of saints (male and female), the Man of Sorrows with the Instruments of the Passion (Arma Christi), and scenes of the Deposition from the Cross and the Lamentation over the Dead Christ.

THE CHURCH OF ST GILES (KOSTEL SV. JILJÍ)

The history of this church in the Old Town of Prague probably begins in the twelfth century. The building of the Gothic church was initiated by Bishop John IV of Dražice, as is attested by his emblem on the façade, and it was finished by Archbishop Ernest of Pardubice. The church was consecrated on 4 May 1371. Its architect drew inspiration from the choirs of Cistercian monasteries, which usually have a nave with aisles and flat ends. Two important figures of fourteenth-century spiritual life in Bohemia were preachers at St Giles': John Milíč of Kroměříž and St John Nepomucene. The chapter ceased to exist in 1420. Though the church was remodelled in the Baroque style, some features from the first half of the fourteenth century have been preserved, including, on the south side, a Gothic portal with stylized foliate capitals and a fragment of a wall painting in the west bay with the subject of St Lawrence.

The Church of St Anne was built from 1319 to 1330 at
the instigation of King John and his wife Elizabeth.
Until 1365 it bore the name St Lawrence and served
as a convent sanctuary of Dominican nuns. It took the
place of two buildings that used to stand here – the
Romanesque rotunda of St Lawrence and the commandery
of the Templars, which the Hospitallers had acquired
in 1312 and sold the next year. In addition to funds from
the king and queen, the financing of the convent
building from 1325 to 1329 was provided by the Lords of
Říčany, and a court assessor by the name of Conrad from
Litoměřice is mentioned in 1339 as a donor. The coats
of arms of the convent patrons still decorate the bosses
of the vault, which is today in the Lapidarium (the stone
sculpture collection) of the National Museum, Prague.
The church was built in two stages. After 1313, work
began on the nave with a large gallery for the nuns, who
were still holding their services in the earlier Church of
St Lawrence. In the initial stage, the nave and the first two
bays of the choir were built and vaulted. In the second
stage (c.1360), another lodge, using a simplified set of
architectural forms, enclosed the elegant choir. The rafters
of the church roof are original, dating, as was revealed
by dendrochronological research, from 1364. The choir
was decorated in the 1370s and 1380s with remarkable
wall paintings of the Adoration of the Magi, the Allegory
of the Seven Sacraments, and the Entombment (the
Lamentation over the Dead Christ), which all manifest
the clear influence of artists of the court, particularly
Theodoric of Prague and the Master of the Třeboň
Altarpiece.

Adoration of the Magi – north wall of the presbytery.

Allegory of the Seven Sacraments – north wall of the presbytery.

The Entombment/The Lamentation over the Dead Christ – south wall of the presbytery.

PRAGUE CROSSROADS, ST ANNE'S

As part of the Emperor Joseph II's suppression of the monasteries, the convent and its Church of St Anne were closed down in 1782, and were thereafter used for various non-religious purposes, including housing. In 1999 the church was leased by the Dagmar and Václav Havel Foundation VIZE 97 for a new international cultural centre called the Prague Crossroads (Pražská křižovatka), which opened after the reconstruction of the church in 2004.

28/ THE CHURCH OF ST MARTIN (KOSTEL SV. MARTINA)

Beginning as the parish church of a settlement called Újezd svatého Martina, St Martin's was built from 1178 to 1187. In the 1230s, the settlement was divided in two by the new walls of the Old Town of Prague. Its smaller part, with the Church of St Martin, which was built right up against the town wall (hence its full name, Church of St Martin in the Wall), became part of the city; its larger part remained outside the walls. The church was completely rebuilt from 1350 to 1358. The enlarged nave was covered with rib vaults; a presbytery was built with a flat end and a pair of windows, and was covered with groined vaulting. Its ribs spring from pyramidal corbels decorated with human faces. The bosses are decorated with roses and stars, both of which are Marian symbols. Today's appearance of the church is the result of purist rebuilding carried out by Kamil Hilbert from 1905 to 1908.

29A–D/ THE CHURCH OF OUR LADY OF THE SNOW (KOSTEL PANNY MARIE SNĚŽNÉ)

This monastery church of Carmelite friars is dedicated to Our Lady of the Snow. It was meant to be the largest church in the New Town of Prague. Charles IV founded it in 1347, the day after his coronation as King of Bohemia. For the rafters of the church he donated wood from the dais on which the coronation banquet was held. The church was intended as a three-aisled basilica. The high choir, with five narrow bays of vaulting, has an apse comprising five sides of a dodecagon, and there was a chapel (today only ruins) attached to the choir. When the church was finally consecrated in 1397 it was still not vaulted. The grandly conceived three-aisled basilican church was in fact never completed. The linearity of the 'post-classic' style, that is, late High Gothic, is typical of the construction of this church. The lodge of the late Matthew of Arras may have helped to build it.

(149)

TYMPANUM FROM THE PLANNED PORTAL OF OUR LADY OF THE SNOW

The high reliefs of what is called the 'tympanum' (*c*.1350) come from the great tower. They were made to commemorate the coronation of Charles IV and Blanche of Valois in 1347. Whereas, originally, the reliefs on the tower were divided by cornices into three stages, today on the tympanum the first and second registers are united. Originally, on the lower right, Charles IV was kneeling with the emblem of the King of the Romans, and on the left, his wife Blanche of Valois was kneeling with the emblem of Bohemia. Between them kneeled Carmelite friars. On the second stage was a high relief showing the Coronation of the Virgin. Surrounded by a halo of sunshine, she was enthroned on a lion – a reference to Mary as the Throne of Solomon (or the Seat of Wisdom) and to the emblem of Queen Blanche. She is crowned by Christ mounted on an eagle, an allusion to the emblem of Charles IV. The rose bushes behind the two figures are symbols of heaven. Between the two figures is the trunk of the Tree of Life 'growing' into the third register, where the subject of the Trinity dominates.

Ruins of the chapel attached to the north side of the choir of Our Lady of the Snow.

30/ THE TOWN HALL OF THE NEW TOWN (NOVOMĚSTSKÁ RADNICE)

The location and size of the town hall correspond to the importance of the New Town of Prague. The original town hall, in nearby Řeznická ulice, was soon too small to meet the requirements of the New Town officials, and a new town hall was built, from 1377 to 1398, on the north side of Karlovo náměstí (Charles Square, formerly the Cattle Market). Its earliest part is the east block of buildings in Vodičkova ulice. After 1411, a south wing was built with its façade on Karlovo náměstí. The large two-aisled council hall, comprising six bays of vaulting supported by two cylindrical piers, is among the most beautiful secular spaces of Luxembourg Prague.

The appearance of the town hall today, particularly the façade on Karlovo náměstí, is the result of remodelling from 1520 to 1526 and also after the fire of 1559.

31A–K/ THE EMMAUS ABBEY (EMAUZSKÝ KLÁŠTER ALSO KNOWN AS NA SLOVANECH)

The abbey of Slav Benedictines, which is called Emmaus, was founded by Charles IV next to the ancient parish Church of Cosmas and Damian on 21 November 1347. In order to further the Slavonic liturgy and culture, monks were sent here from the Dalmatian island of Pašman near Zadar. The abbey was consecrated to the Virgin Mary and the Slav patron saints: Cyril and Methodius, Procopius, Adalbert, and Jerome. From this abbey comes, by a circuitous route, part of the Reims Gospel, some of which is written in the Glagolitic alphabet (another part was written in Cyrillic in Kievan Rus'). Mistakenly believed to be a manuscript of St Jerome's, it was used for oath-taking in the coronation of the kings of France at Reims Cathedral until the end of the seventeenth century. The abbey church is a unique piece of architecture of the Danubian type.

It is based on a ground plan of a hall church of two
aisles and a nave of seven bays. The nave and aisles each
terminate in a five-sided apse. The sedile on the south wall
of the southernmost apse is decorated with the emblem of
the Empire and of Bohemia. Originally, the church was
sumptuously decorated with wall paintings. All that has been
preserved is the reconstructed heraldic emblems on the vault
and a fragment of a wall painting in the south aisle, which
shows St Benedict. Attached to the church are a cloister with
wall paintings and what is known as the Imperial Chapel.

The wall paintings in the cloister were made from 1358 to 1362 by painters working for Charles IV at Karlstein Castle. The whole cycle, adorning all of the cloister walls and, most probably, also the walls of the Imperial Chapel, is based on typological parallelism, that is, scenes from the Old Testament are related to New Testament figures and events as their prototypes. The whole cycle represents the history of Christ's Salvation: it begins on the south wall of the cloister with the Fall of Man, that is, Original Sin, and ends here with the Annunciation, that is, the beginning of the years of Grace. It continues in the west wing with stories of Christ's childhood, and ends with His baptism, that is, the beginning of His public activity, which is depicted in the north wing. The highpoint on this wall is Christ's Entry into Jerusalem. Considering the absence of Passion subject matter in the east wing, it is fair to assume that such scenes were located in the Imperial Chapel. The series originally ended in the east wing of the cloister with scenes of Christ in Glory.

Sedile on the south wall of the apse.

The Annunciation; Moses in front of the Burning Bush; Gideon with the fleece.

Judith of the Old Testament.

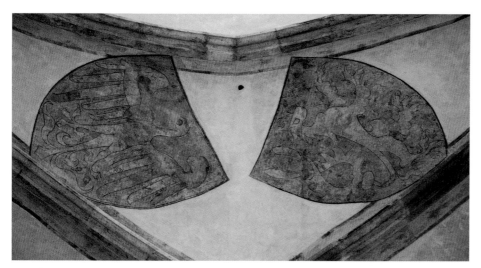

On the left, an escutcheon with the emblem of Rome; on the right, an escutcheon with the emblem of Bohemia.

On the left, an escutcheon with the emblem of Silesia; on the right, an escutcheon with the emblem of St Wenceslas.

On the left, an escutcheon with the emblem of Moravia; on the right an escutcheon with the emblem of the archbishop of Prague.

Legend of St Benedict – south aisle, detail.

Corbels on the north portal of the nave. →

32/ THE STEEPLES OF THE CHURCHES OF ST APOLLINARIS AND ST CATHERINE

The hill called Větrov, which became part of the New Town of Prague in 1348, is dominated by the Church of St Apollinaris. Seen from Vyšehrad, the steeple of St Apollinaris' appears next to the similarly slender steeple of the Church of St Catherine.

The Church of St Catherine was founded by the Emperor and King, Charles IV, in 1355, as the convent church of the Order of Augustinian nuns. It was dedicated to St Catherine to commemorate the victory of the young Charles IV at the Battle of San Felice, fought on St Catherine's Day, 25 November 1332. The convent and the church were badly damaged by the Hussites in 1420. All that remains of the medieval architecture today is the high tower. The convent church was remodelled in the Baroque style from 1737 to 1741.

This church was built in two stages. The first was from 1360
to 1367, when the nave was built in the form of a great hall
covered with five bays of groin vault and a saddleback roof
surmounted by a flèche (the ridge turret). Next, in the second
quarter of the fourteenth century, the narrow presbytery and
steeple were built. The nave is decorated with wall paintings,
from c.1380, with the subject matter of the Giving of the
Keys (*Traditio Clavium*), the Virgin with women saints, and
St Wenceslas. The church was the seat of the chapter, which
was moved here from Sadská (37 km east of Prague), in 1362,
with the consent of the first Archbishop of Prague, Ernest of
Pardubice.

The wall paintings in the aisles are linked with the reform ideas of John of Jenstein, the third Archbishop of Prague. On the south wall, we see Christ handing the Keys of the Kingdom of Heaven to St Peter. They are accompanied by the other eleven Apostles – all are standing on Old Testament prophets and holding banderoles (speech scrolls) with the Apostles' Creed. This is a reference to John of Jenstein's *Tractatulus de potestate clavium* (A little tract on the power of the Keys), in which he reacts to the Papal Schism. The Apostles standing on the Prophets indicate that the Old Testament foreshadows the New. On the north wall is the figure of St Wenceslas with angels, the Virgin Mary, Sts Anne, Mary Magdalene, Catherine, and other female saints. Like the Apostles on the opposite wall, the figures are portrayed standing either on their destroyers (for example, St Wenceslas on the figure of his pagan brother Boleslaus) or on their companions (the Virgin stands on St Joseph). Each of the figures on both walls is elongated, ethereal.

34/ THE CHURCH OF THE ASSUMPTION AND THE BLESSED CHARLEMAGNE (KOSTEL NANEBEVZETÍ PANNY MARIE A SV. KARLA VELIKÉHO)

Charles IV was very fond of the Canons Regular, priests living under the Rule of St Augustine, and so on top of the Prague hill now known as Karlov, in 1350, he founded the canonry with the Church of the Assumption and the Blessed Charlemagne. By his choice of whom the church would be dedicated to and what the central plan for its nave would be, Charles intended this church to make reference to the central chapel in the Königspfalz at Aix-la-Chapelle (Aachen), which had been built by Charlemagne, and where the Kings of the Romans, including Charles, were crowned. The construction of the whole complex with the church took place from 1350 to 1377. A short, narrow presbytery was attached to the octagonal nave, which in Charles's time was not yet vaulted. By analogy it is reasonable to assume that the nave was originally meant to be vaulted on four piers.

35/ THE CHURCH OF THE ANNUNCIATION (KOSTEL ZVĚSTOVÁNÍ PANNY MARIE NA SLUPI/ NA TRÁVNÍČKU)

Monks of the Servite Order (Friar Servants of Mary), which was founded in Florence, were settled in the valley of the Botič stream, *c.*1360, by the Emperor Charles IV. In the third quarter of the fourteen century, the delicate building of this church consecrated to Our Lady of Humility was erected beside the friary. The nave is square, its vault rests on a central pier, and a slender steeple rises up on the west façade. Considering whom the church is consecrated to, it is fair to assume that the painting of the *Madonna of Humility*, also known as the *Vyšehrad Madonna* or *Madonna of the Rain* (see pp. 178–79), may have come from here.

36/ THE CHURCH OF ST STEPHEN
(KOSTEL SV. ŠTĚPÁNA)

Charles IV founded this church together with the New Town of Prague as the parish church of the upper part of the town. Its consecration to St Stephen was adopted from the nearby rotunda, which was then consecrated to St Longinus. In rough form, the building was finished by 1374, and was completed, including its tower on the west façade, just before the Hussite Wars. The church is a three-aisled basilica. It has a short but wide nave, comprised of four bays with ribbed groin vaults, and a presbytery, which is covered with two bays of ribbed groin vaulting and terminates in a five-sided apse.

37/ THE CHURCH OF SAINTS HENRY AND CUNIGUNDE (KOSTEL SV. JINDŘICHA A SV. KUNHUTY)

This church, built in the late fourteenth century at the same time as the Church of St Stephen, was the main parish church of the New Town. It was consecrated to St Henry II (the Holy Roman Emperor and a Luxembourg) and St Cunigunde (his wife) because they were buried in Bamberg, Bavaria, and the visiting bishops of Bamberg were archbishops of Prague. This is a three-aisled hall church with four vaulted bays. Attached to the nave is a long choir of two vaulted bays, with a five-sided apse. The church has a tower built into the south-west bay of the three-aisled vessel. Construction work dragged on until the fifteenth century.

(174)

38/ THE CHURCH OF ST WENCESLAS IN ZDERAZ (KOSTEL SV. VÁCLAVA NA ZDERAZE)

The original church, a simple single-aisled structure with an apse, was built by the Order of the Holy Sepulchre (a crusading Order attached to the Augustinians) in the twelfth century, and they consecrated it to St Wenceslas. Zderaz is the name of a settlement that vanished after the founding of the New Town, which is also when the Church of St Wenceslas became a parish church. It was rebuilt, probably from 1350 to 1379, because in the visitation records of 1379–82 it is described as nicely built, with four altars inside. The choir and its polygonal apse, covered with two bays of groin vaulting, were probably completed by then, but before the nave was vaulted, it was given a temporary roof, and it seems that it was meant to have a two-aisled hall form. Fragments of wall paintings have been preserved in the presbytery. Illustrating the Virgin Birth, the Annunciation, and Christ crucified on the Tree of Life, these wall paintings have been plausibly dated to the beginning of the fifteenth century.

39/ VYŠEHRAD WITH THE BASILICA OF SAINTS PETER AND PAUL

The Vyšehrad hill fort, spread out on a cliff above the right bank of the River Vltava, is accompanied by many legends about the earliest history of Bohemia. The first evidence of the existence of Vyšehrad comes from the second half of the tenth century. Vyšehrad was developed by Vratislav II (*reg.* 1061–92), the first King of Bohemia. After disputes with his brother Jaromír, who was the bishop of Prague, he moved his seat to Vyšehrad and, in 1070, founded here, at the Basilica of Sts Peter and Paul, the royal chapter of canons led by a prior. In 1144, Pope Lucius II granted the prior of Vyšehrad exemption from the authority of the bishop, which meant that he was subject only to the Roman Curia of the Holy See. Vyšehrad, which had a close link to the Přemyslids historically, was granted an important place in the coronation ceremony by Charles IV (who was descended from the Přemyslids on his mother's side). On the eve of the coronation, the future king was required to go to Vyšehrad, where he received the satchel and put on the bast shoes which allegedly belonged to the founder of the dynasty, Přemysl the Ploughman.

40/ *THE VYŠEHRAD MADONNA* (*MADONNA OF THE RAIN*)

This painting probably comes from the collegiate church of Sts Peter and Paul at Vyšehrad, or possibly from the Servite Church of Our Lady of Humility below Vyšehrad (kostel Panny Marie Pokorné, now known as the kostel Zvěstování Panny Marie Na Trávníčku or Na Slupi – the Church of the Annunciation or Our Lady of Humility, see pp. 168–69), which was founded by the Emperor and King, Charles IV. At the end of the sixteenth century, the painting became part of the collections of Rudolph II and from there ended up at Vyšehrad, where it was venerated as miraculous during the Baroque period. It is the type of depiction of the Virgin known as the Madonna of Humility, very popular in Italy (Santa Madonna dell'Umilita). Sitting on a green lawn with flowers, she is clothed in a blue robe and is nursing the Christ Child. She is wearing a crown (or a halo) with twelve stars, a reference to the Woman of the Apocalypse, and has a crescent moon under her feet, a reference to the Assumption. The painting, from *c*.1360, is very likely a copy of a devotional painting (not preserved), a miraculous image by Simone Martini, and was probably a gift from the Prior of Vyšehrad, Wenceslas Králík of Buřenice. The background of the painting was originally a panel covered with silver gilt and imprinted with a repeating decoration of crossed keys (the emblem of the Vyšehrad chapter) and lions (the emblem of the Kingdom of Bohemia).

(179)

WHO WAS CHARLES IV?

The son of John of Luxembourg and Elizabeth of Bohemia, he was born on 14 May 1316, and was baptized Wenceslas. He was called Charles at his confirmation in France, after his godfather, Charles IV, the King of France, called the Fair, at whose court he was brought up. He returned to Bohemia in 1333, and began his reign on 11 May 1346. But he was not crowned King of Bohemia until a year later, on 2 September 1347, even though he had been crowned King of the Romans already on 26 January 1346. He was crowned the Emperor of the Holy Roman Empire on 5 April 1355. That same year he was also crowned the Lombard King (King of Italy) and, in 1365, the ruler of the Kingdom of Arles. He died in Prague on 29 November 1378, and was buried in St Vitus' Cathedral.

On the basis of research of the remains of Charles IV, conducted under the direction of the paleoanthropologist and physician Emanuel Vlček in 1976, it appears that Charles IV was an athletic type with a strong frame, which had been formed by intentional physical exercise and riding. He was between 172.5 and 173.5 cm in height. But his true height was considerably distorted by thoracic kyphosis (forward curvature of the upper back). From Charles's vertebrae it has been deduced that he also suffered from scoliosis. He was, for his time, above average height, but probably appeared about three centimetres shorter. In his youth he was very lively and never missed an opportunity to duel or joust. He participated in tournaments under an assumed name and coat of arms. He liked wild clothes, and at balls and entertainments he ostentatiously courted burgher women. Reports of his transgressions travelled as far as Avignon, and Pope Clement VI sharply reproached his pupil and friend Charles for this conduct:

> From the reports of many people, we have learnt that some German magnates, to whom your honour is truly dear, are complaining and can hardly bear, that you, by your clothes, which you wear too short and too closefitting, do not preserve the dignity that belongs to the supreme honour of emperor, and that, contrary to what behoves that dignity, you take part in jousting and tournaments. We, who out of fatherly love desire the increase of your honour, have been astonished, and emphatically ask your serene highness that in future you wear long and loose-fitting clothes, which would testify to your maturity. It is required of such a great ruler that you give up such jousts and tournaments, and that you show yourself to be dignified and mature in word and deed, so that nothing unfitting or reproachable about you could be observed, but that, instead, you recognize the rank whose insignia and dignity you bear, recognize behaviour, and embody virtuous deeds.

In his research, Vlček discovered that Charles had many healed wounds and injuries. The most serious was probably an injury to his cervical vertebrae, which he received in a tournament. After a hard dull blow with a lance to the left side of his neck, Charles, in full armour, fell from his horse and broke his jaw and injured his cervical vertebrae. Particularly in his later years, Charles suffered from gout, and his reported carving at pieces of wood during audiences was very likely a means of therapy. During his visit to France in 1378, Charles IV suffered a serious attack of gout. According to Pierre d'Orgemont, chancellor to the King of France:

> He rode part of the way in a litter that was harnessed between two mules or borne by bearers. In the palace of the King of France, he was then transferred to a chair, and carried up the stairs at the Basilica of Saint-Denis to pray at the tomb of St Louis and see the relics. Despite his great pain, he rode into Paris on horseback at the side of the King of France, for he was, after all, the Emperor.

The emperor's regimen surely contributed to the progression of this disease, because, as we know, his table was always laden with good drink and roast game. His physicians advised him to drink high-quality wine from the vineyards of the Moselle and Rhine river valleys, rather than the tart local wines of Bohemia. For these reasons, it only makes sense that he founded Carlsbad (Karlovy Vary), because the hot springs had a beneficial effect on his health. The last injury that the Emperor suffered was a fracture of his left femur. This left him bedridden, which then led to pneumonia.

Charles IV was an outstanding intellectual and profoundly pious. He was certainly influenced by two great Christian thinkers, St Augustine and St Thomas Aquinas. From Augustine he adopted the idea that in his (or her) aims each legitimate ruler looks predominantly to God. From Aquinas he took the idea that a ruler should look to his (or her) subjects and their wellbeing in the temporal sense. Charles believed in the sanctifying power of relics, which is why he sought to bring all the important relics of the Christian world to Prague and Karlstein. He based his views on the exegesis of Nicholas of Lyra, who believed that on Judgement Day Christ would descend to where His relics and those of the Virgin were assembled. Charles regarded education highly, and, in addition to Prague University, he founded and supported other university institutions. His outstanding knowledge of languages enabled him to communicate with many people: according to Adalbert Raňkův, for example, Charles spoke and wrote five languages: French, German, Italian, Czech, and Latin. He recorded his thoughts in several literary works in Latin, in particular *Vita Caroli* (his autobiography), *Ordo ad coronandum regem Bohemorum et Ordo ad benedicendam reginam* (the Order of Service of the Coronation), *Hystoria nova de sancto Wenceslao martyre, duce Bohemorum* (a life of St Wenceslas), and *Moralitates* (a collection of philosophical maxims and spiritual writings).

FOREBEARS AND DESCENDANTS OF CHARLES IV

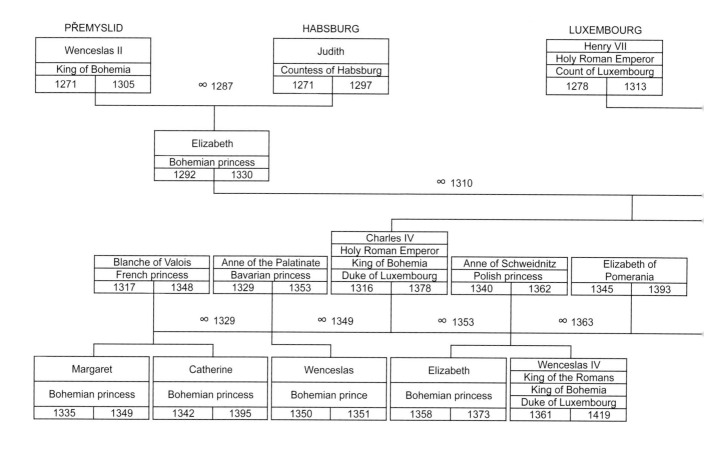

PŘEMYSLID

Wenceslas II	
King of Bohemia	
1271	1305

∞ 1287

HABSBURG

Judith	
Countess of Habsburg	
1271	1297

LUXEMBOURG

Henry VII	
Holy Roman Emperor	
Count of Luxembourg	
1278	1313

Elizabeth	
Bohemian princess	
1292	1330

∞ 1310

Blanche of Valois	
French princess	
1317	1348

Anne of the Palatinate	
Bavarian princess	
1329	1353

Charles IV	
Holy Roman Emperor	
King of Bohemia	
Duke of Luxembourg	
1316	1378

Anne of Schweidnitz	
Polish princess	
1340	1362

Elizabeth of	
Pomerania	
1345	1393

∞ 1329   ∞ 1349   ∞ 1353   ∞ 1363

Margaret	
Bohemian princess	
1335	1349

Catherine	
Bohemian princess	
1342	1395

Wenceslas	
Bohemian prince	
1350	1351

Elizabeth	
Bohemian princess	
1358	1373

Wenceslas IV	
King of the Romans	
King of Bohemia	
Duke of Luxembourg	
1361	1419

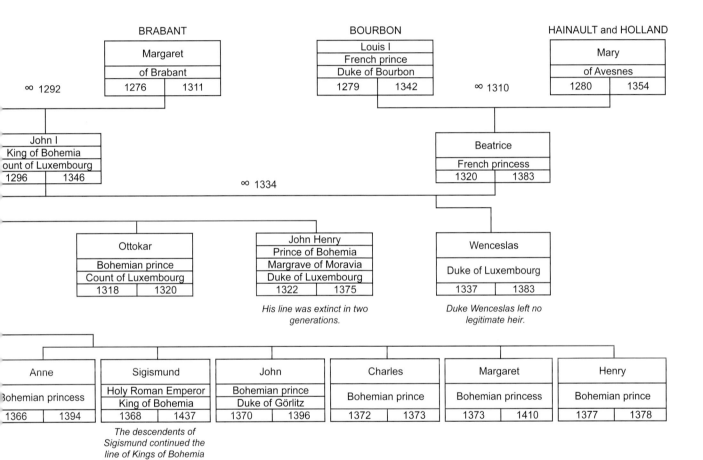

BRABANT

Margaret	
of Brabant	
1276	1311

∞ 1292

BOURBON

Louis I	
French prince	
Duke of Bourbon	
1279	1342

∞ 1310

HAINAULT and HOLLAND

Mary	
of Avesnes	
1280	1354

John I	
King of Bohemia	
Count of Luxembourg	
1296	1346

∞ 1334

Beatrice	
French princess	
1320	1383

Ottokar	
Bohemian prince	
Count of Luxembourg	
1318	1320

John Henry	
Prince of Bohemia	
Margrave of Moravia	
Duke of Luxembourg	
1322	1375

*His line was extinct in two
generations.*

Wenceslas	
Duke of Luxembourg	
1337	1383

*Duke Wenceslas left no
legitimate heir.*

Anne	
Bohemian princess	
1366	1394

Sigismund	
Holy Roman Emperor	
King of Bohemia	
1368	1437

*The descendents of
Sigismund continued the
line of Kings of Bohemia
until 1918.*

John	
Bohemian prince	
Duke of Görlitz	
1370	1396

Charles	
Bohemian prince	
1372	1373

Margaret	
Bohemian princess	
1373	1410

Henry	
Bohemian prince	
1377	1378

Drawn up by *Petr Nohel*

(183)

EMINENT PERSONS OF CHARLES IV'S DAY AND LATER

Anne of Bavaria (of the Palatinate, 1329–1353), second wife of Charles IV, daughter of Rudolph II, Count Palatine of the Rhine, and Anne of Carinthia. She bore him a son, Wenceslas, who died at the age of two.

Anne of Schweidnitz (Anna Świdnicka, 1339–1362), third wife of Charles IV, daughter of Henry II, Duke of Schweidnitz, and Catherine, a Hungarian princess. Brought up at the Hungarian royal court. In 1358, she gave birth to Elizabeth and, three years later, Wenceslas IV.

Blanche of Valois (1316–1348) (baptized Marguerite), first wife of Charles IV, daughter of Charles of Valois and Mahaut of Châtillon, and sister of Philip VI of France. Joined her husband in Prague in 1334; a year later a daughter, Margaret, was born to them, followed, in 1342, by another daughter, Catherine.

Elizabeth of Bohemia (Eliška Přemyslovna, 1292–1330), mother of Charles IV, and wife of John of Luxembourg. Was the last Přemyslid.

Elizabeth of Pomerania (Eliška Pomořanská, 1346–1393), fourth wife of Charles IV, daughter of Bogislaw V, Duke of Pomerania, and his wife, Elizabeth, daughter of Casimir III, King of Poland. Bore Charles six children: Anne (1366–1394; Queen of England), Sigismund (1368–1437; King of Hungary, Holy Roman Emperor, King of Bohemia), John (1370–1396; Duke of Görlitz and Margrave of Brandenburg), Charles (1372–1373), Margaret (1373–1410; Burgravine of Nuremberg), and Henry (1377–1378).

John of Luxembourg (1296–1346), father of Charles IV, was the son of Henry VII (Count of Luxembourg, King of the Romans, and first Emperor of the House of Luxembourg), and Margaret, daughter of John of Brabant and niece of Philip IV of France. Died at the Battle of Crécy, in 1346, and went into legend as one of the last knight-kings of Europe.

Sigismund of Luxembourg (1368–1437), son of Charles IV and Elizabeth of Pomerania, crowned King of Hungary in 1387, King of Bohemia in 1414, and Emperor in 1433. Through his daughter Elizabeth (his only child), who married Albrecht of Habsburg, he was grandfather to Ladislaus the Posthumous and Elizabeth of Habsburg, wife of Casimir IV Jagiellon, and was therefore the great-grandfather of Vladislaus II of Bohemia and Hungary.

Wenceslas IV (1361–1419), son of Charles IV and Anne of Schweidnitz, successor to Charles IV as King of Bohemia since the age of two, and, in 1376, King of the Romans. In 1370, married Joanna of Bavaria, and, in 1389, Sophia of Bavaria. Both marriages were childless.

Anne (1366–1394), daughter of Charles IV and Elizabeth of Pomerania, wife of the Richard II Plantagenet, King of England.

Catherine (1342–?), daughter of Charles IV and Blanche of Valois, married Rudolf IV of Habsburg, Duke of Austria, and, after his death, Otto V of Bavaria.

Henry VII of Luxembourg (1275–1313), father of John of Luxembourg.

Joanna of Bavaria (1362–1386), wife of Wenceslas IV.

John Henry of Luxembourg (1322–1375), younger brother of Charles IV, Count of Tyrol, Margrave of Moravia, father of the Margrave Jobst of Moravia.

Margaret (1335–1349), daughter of Charles IV and Blanche of Valois, married Louis I, King of Hungary.

Adalbert (Vojtěch) Raňkův of Ježov (*c*.1320–1388), theologian and scholar, attended the University of Paris, where he also served as rector; was also active at Oxford.

Agnes of Bohemia (1205/11–1282), daughter of Ottokar II Přemysl, cofounded (with her brother, Wenceslas II) the Franciscan friary in the Old Town (1233) and initiated the Order of the Knights of the Cross with the Red Star (1252). Beatified in 1874, canonized in 1989.

Albert I (1347–1404), Duke of Bavaria.

Albert of Sternberg (*c*.1333–1380), Bishop of Litomyšl, Archbishop of Magdeburg.

Angelo of Florence (?–?), Italian apothecary who settled in Prague, was court apothecary to Charles IV, founded a physic garden next to his shop in 1374.

Baldwin of Luxembourg (1285–1354), brother of the Emperor Henry VII, from 1308 onwards, Archbishop of Trier, Elector, great uncle of Charles IV.

Bořivoj II (*c*.1064–1124), Duke of Bohemia (*reg*. 1100–07, 1117–20), a Přemyslid, son of Vratislav II (Duke and later first King of Bohemia), younger half-brother of Bretislaus II.

Bretislaus I (Břetislav I, 1002/05–1055), Duke of Bohemia (ruled in Moravia from 1029 and in Bohemia from 1034, until his death), of the Přemyslid dynasty, illegitimate son of Oldřich, Duke of Bohemia, and his low-born concubine Božena.

Bretislaus (Břetislav II, *reg*.1092–1100), Duke of Bohemia, of the Přemyslid dynasty, son of Vratislav II (first King of Bohemia), and elder half-brother of Bořivoj II.

Casimir III the Great (1310–1370), king of Poland.

Charles IV the Fair (1294–1328), King of France, last Direct Capetian King of France; uncle and godfather of Charles IV of Luxembourg.

Charles V the Wise (1338–1380), King of France from the Valois dynasty.

Charles of Valois (1270–1325), brother of Philip IV of France; father-in-law of Charles IV of Luxembourg.

Claretus (Bartoloměj z Chlumce, called Mistr Klaret in Czech, *c*.1320–1370), probably one of the first students of Prague University, a canon of St Vitus' Cathedral, the initiator and main compiler of the Latin-Czech encyclopaedic dictionary.

Clement VI (1291–1352) born Pierre Roger, elected pope in 1342, had his seat in Avignon; was a patron of the arts, a teacher of Charles IV.

Cola di Rienzo (1313/14–1354), Italian humanist, gifted orator and politician who pushed for reform in Rome.

Elizabeth Richeza (in Czech, Eliška/Alžběta Rejčka and, in Polish, Ryksa Elżbieta, 1280–1335), daughter of Przemysł II of Poland, and wife of Wenceslas II and, after his death, Rudolph of Habsburg; was a donor of illuminated manuscripts.

Ernest of Pardubice (Arnošt z Pardubic, *c*.1297–1364), first Archbishop of Prague, the last Bishop of Prague.

Gall of Strahov (Havel ze Strahova, Gallus de Monte Sion, first quarter of the 14th century–*c*.1388), court physician to Charles IV, taught at Prague University.

Giotto (1266/7–1337), Italian painter, sculptor, and architect of the Early Renaissance.

Günther of Schwarzburg (1304–1349), anti-king to Charles IV.

Henry of Bohemia (Henry of Carinthia, Heinrich von Kärnten, c.1265–1335), Duke of Carinthia, Count of Tyrol, married Anne of Bohemia (the first of his three wives), daughter of Wenceslas II. Was King of Bohemia in 1306 and again from 1307 to 1310.

Henry the Fowler (876–936), King of the Romans, Duke of Saxony, founder of the Ottonian Dynasty of monarchs of the Holy Roman Empire.

Hilbert, Kamil (1869–1933), architect and restorer, and, after the death of Josef Mocker, chief architect of the completion of St Vitus' Cathedral (finished in 1929).

Huss, John (Jan Hus; c.1369–1415), priest, preacher, religious thinker, and reformer; in 1409–10, was Rector of Prague University; sentenced to death at the Council of Constance, and burnt at the stake as a heretic.

Jacobellus of Mies (Jakoubek ze Stříbra, c.1375–1429), preacher, friend of John Huss, and early proponent of receiving Communion in both kinds.

John IV of Dražice (Jan IV z Dražic, 1301–1343), Bishop of Prague.

John of Jenstein (Jan z Jenštejna, between 1347and 1350–1400), cleric, artist, chancellor to King Wenceslas IV from 1373 to 1384, and third Archbishop of Prague from 1379 to 1396.

John of Neumarkt (Jan ze Středy, 1310–1380) chancellor of Charles IV, Bishop of Litomyšl and Olomouc, man of letters, translator, and patron of the arts.

Krabice of Weitmühle, Benedict (Beneš Krabice z Veitmile, ?–1375), Prague canon and chronicler.

Králík of Buřenice, Wenceslas (Václav Králík z Buřenic, c.1345–1416), distinguished prelate and patron of the arts.

Kranner, Joseph (1801–1871), architect of the Romantic period and early revival styles, took part, from 1859 until his death, in the completion of St Vitus' Cathedral.

Louis I (1326–1382), King of Hungary and Poland.

Louis IV the Bavarian (1282/7–1347), Emperor of the Holy Roman Empire.

Martini, Simone (1284–1344), Italian painter of Gothic frescos and panel paintings.

Master of the Krumlov Madonna (*fl.* late fourteenth century), sculptor of the Gothic period, active in Bohemia, a leading artist of the so-called International Gothic (in German, the *Weicher Stil* or *Schöner Stil*).

Master of the Michle Madonna (*fl.* 1325–50), a leading Bohemian sculptor.

Master Oswald (?–1383), a painter of the High Gothic active in Prague from 1356 to 1380, known particularly for his wall paintings.

Master of the Vyšebrod Altar (*fl.* 1340s to 1350s), a painter of the High Gothic period, employed in the service of Charles IV.

Matthew of Arras (1290–1352), first architect of St Vitus' Cathedral, summoned to Prague by Charles IV.

Milič of Kroměříž, John (Jan Milíč z Kroměříže, after 1320–1374) originally a notary in the service of Charles IV; after his departure from the royal chancery became a preacher and promoter of Church reform. Died in Avignon.

Mocker, Josef (1835–1899), Czech architect specialized in the restoration of historic buildings; in 1873 was appointed chief architect to take over from the late Joseph Kranner to complete the building of St Vitus'.

Očko of Vlašim, John (Jan Očko z Vlašimi, ?–1380), second Archbishop of Prague; notary and confident of Charles IV; patron of the arts.

Ottokar I Přemysl (1155/1167–1230), first hereditary king of Bohemia.

Ottokar II Přemysl (c.1233–1278), king of Bohemia, from the house of Přemyslid, called the King of Iron and Gold.

Parler, Peter (1332/33–1399), master mason and sculptor, summoned to Prague from Swabia by Charles IV; was principal architect of St Vitus' Cathedral.

Petrarch (Francesco Petrarca) (1304–1374), Italian poet and scholar, early humanist, sometimes called Father of the Renaissance.

Philip VI (1293–1350), from the house of Valois, King of France.

Přemysl the Ploughman (Přemysl Oráč) (?–?), together with Princess Libuše, was the legendary founder of the Přemyslid dynasty of dukes and kings of Bohemia.

Roger, Pierre see Clement VI.

Rudolph I (1284–1356), Duke of Saxe-Wittenberg and the first Elector of Saxony, backed Charles IV.

Rudolph II (1306–1353), Count Palatine of the Rhine, called 'the Blind', father of Anne of Bavaria (Anne of the Palatinate), second wife of Charles IV.

Rudolph II of Habsburg (1552–1612), King of Bohemia, King of Hungary, King of Croatia, Archduke of Austria, Emperor of the Holy Roman Empire, with his seat at Prague Castle.

Rudolph IV of Habsburg (1339–1365), Duke of Austria and Carinthia, Count of Tyrol, son-in-law of Charles IV (as husband of Charles's daughter, Catherine of Luxembourg).

Semitecolo, Niccolò (Nicoletto), *fl.* 1353–72, Italian painter.

Spytihněv II (1031–1061), Duke of Bohemia from the house of Přemyslid.

Theodoric of Prague (?–1381?), a court painter to Charles IV, renowned artist of the wall paintings in the Chapel of the Holy Cross, Karlstein.

Tomaso da Modena (1326–1379), Italian painter who also worked for Charles IV outside Bohemia.

Urban V (1310–1370), Pope from 1362 to 1370.

Urban VI (*c.*1318–1389), Pope from 1378 to 1389, first pope of the Western Schism.

Velislav (?–1367), notary and chancellor of John of Luxembourg and Charles IV; probably commissioned the Paupers' Bible known as the *Velislai biblia picta*.

Vladislav II Jagiellon (1456–1516), son of Casimir IV of Poland and Elizabeth of Habsburg (the granddaughter of Sigismund of Luxembourg), King of Bohemia as of 1471 and of Hungary as of 1490).

Waldhauser, Conrad (*c.*1326–1369), preacher, writer, and Church reformer, active in Prague from 1363 onward.

Wenceslas I (907–935 or possibly 929), Duke of Bohemia from the house of Přemyslid, a principal patron saint of the Bohemian Lands and symbol of Bohemian statehood.

Wenceslas II (Václav II; 1271–1305), King of Bohemia, a Přemyslid, father of Elizabeth of Bohemia.

Wenceslas of Radetz (Václav z Radče; ?– *c.*1481), canon of the chapter of St Vitus' Cathedral, last Clerk of Works there.

Wurmser of Strasbourg, Nicholas (?–?), painter at the court of Charles IV, from at least 1357 to 1360; generally considered to have helped decorate the walls at Karlstein and at Emmaus Abbey.

A MAP OF PRAGUE

1. Prague Castle (Pražský hrad)
2. Cathedral of Sts Vitus, Wenceslas, and Adalbert (chrám sv. Víta, Václava a Vojtěcha)
3. Bishop's Court (Biskupský dvůr), tower, Mostecká no. 16, courtyard of the Three Golden Bells (dům U Tří zlatých zvonků)
4. Church of St Mary under the Chain (kostel Panny Marie pod řetězem), Lázeňská no. 2
5. Hunger Wall (Hladová zeď)
6. Charles Bridge (Karlův most)
7. Bridge Tower on the Old Town side (Staroměstská mostecká věž)
8. Town Hall of the Old Town (Staroměstská radnice), Staroměstské náměstí no. 1
9. Thein Church (chrám Panny Marie [or Matky Boží] před Týnem, Týnský chrám), Staroměstské náměstí
10. Stone Bell House (dům U Kamenného zvonu)
11. Carolinum (Karolinum), Ovocný trh 1/5
12. Church of the Holy Spirit (kostel sv. Ducha), Dušní ulice
13. Church of St Castulus (kostel sv. Haštala), Haštalská ulice
14. Church of St Anne (kostel sv. Anny), Zlatá ulice (entrance)
15. Church of St Giles (kostel sv. Jiljí), Husova ulice
16. Church of Our Lady of the Snow (kostel Panny Marie Sněžné), Jungmannovo náměstí no. 8
17. Wenceslas Square (Václavské náměstí; formerly, the Horse Market)
18. Haymarket Square (Senovážné náměstí)
19. Town Hall of the New Town (Novoměstská radnice), Karlovo náměstí no. 1
20. Charles Square (Karlovo náměstí, formerly the Cattle Market)
21. Emmaus Abbey (Emauzský klášter, also known as Na Slovanech), Vyšehradská no. 49
22. Church of St Apollinaris (kostel sv. Apolináře), Apolinářská ulice
23. Church of the Assumption and the Blessed Charlemagne at Karlov (kostel Nanebevzetí Panny Marie a sv. Karla Velikého na Karlově), Horská ulice
24. Church of the Madonna of Humility (kostel Panny Marie Na Slupi or kostel Panny Marie Na Slupi na Trávníčku), Na Slupi
25. Church of St Catherine (kostel sv. Kateřiny), Kateřinská ulice
26. Church of St Wenceslas (kostel sv. Václava na Zderaze), on the corner of Resslova and Dittrichova streets
27. Church of St Stephen (kostel sv. Štěpána), Štěpánská ulice
28. Church of Sts Henry and Cunigunde (kostel sv. Jindřicha a sv. Kunhuty), Jindřišská ulice
29. Vyšehrad with the Basilica of Saints Peter and Paul

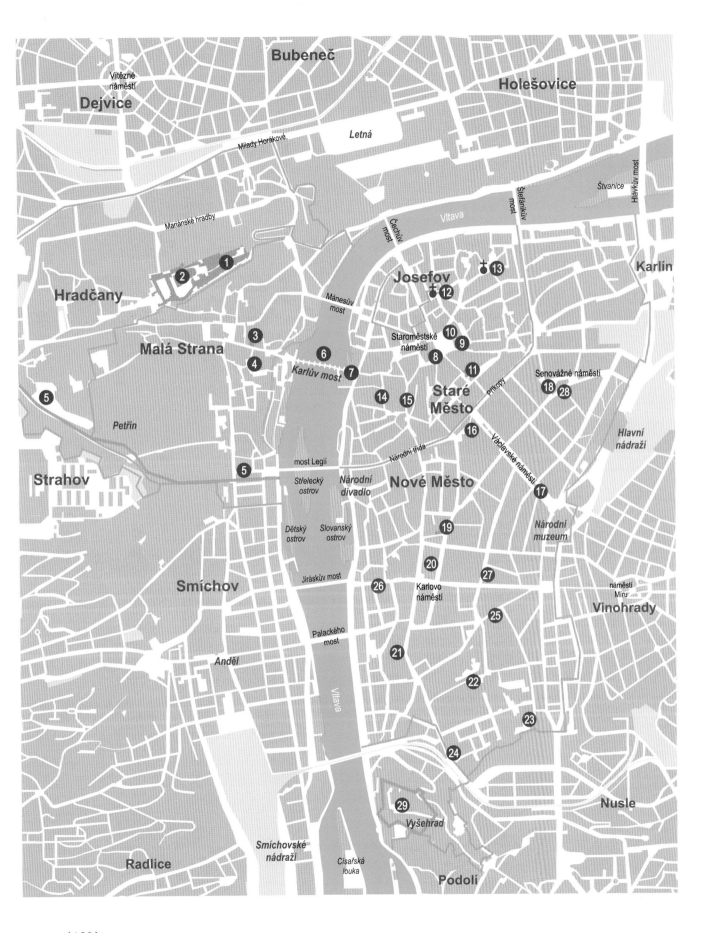

A MAP OF PRAGUE CASTLE

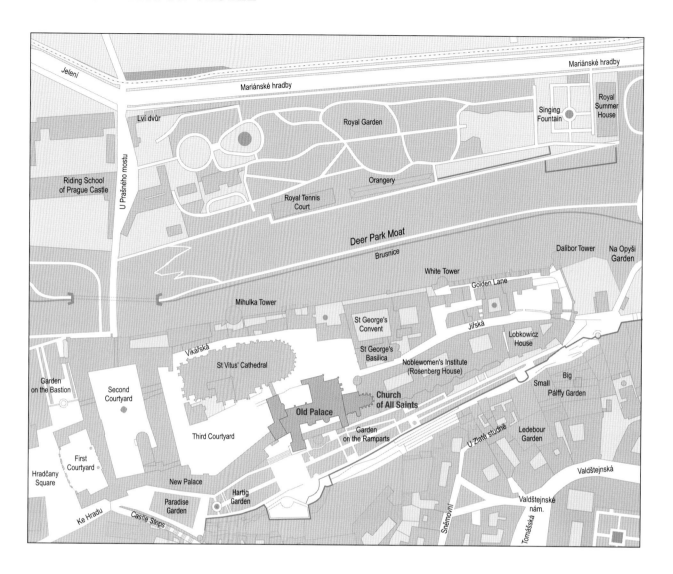

A FLOOR PLAN OF ST VITUS' CATHEDRAL

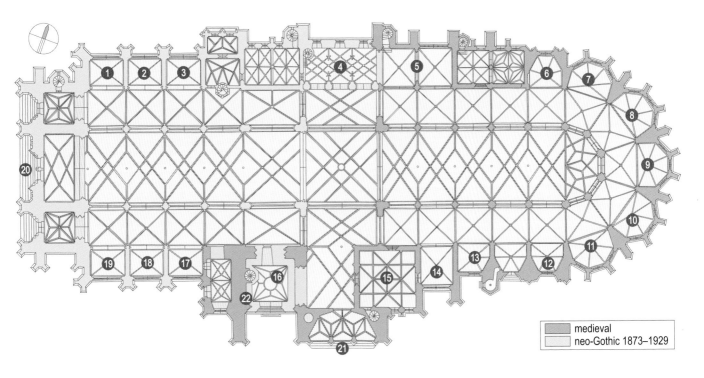

medieval
neo-Gothic 1873–1929

1. Bartoň z Dobenína Chapel
2. Schwarzenberg Chapel
3. Chapel of Provost Hora (also called New Archiepiscopal Chapel)
4. Choir of Bonifaz Wohlmut and Choir Chapel
5. Chapel of St Sigismund
6. Chapel of St Anne (also called Nostitz Chapel)
7. Chapel of the Archbishop (also called Chapel of St Maternus, Pernstein Chapel, Kinský Chapel, Moravian Chapel, Chapel of Cyril and Methodius)
8. Chapel of St John the Baptist (also called Chapel of Ernest of Pardubice, Chapel of St Antony Abbot)
9. Lady Chapel (also called Imperial Chapel, Trinity Chapel, Berka Chapel, Holy Cross Chapel, St Ludmila Chapel)
10. Chapel of the Relics (also called Saxon Chapel, St Adalbert Chapel, St Dorothy Chapel, Sternberg Chapel)
11. Chapel of St John Nepomucene (also called Chapel of Sts Erhard and Odilia, Vlašim Chapel, Chapel of the Visitation)
12. Waldstein Chapel (also called Magdalene Chapel, Sacred Heart Chapel)
13. Holy Cross Chapel (also called Sts Simon and Jude, St Sylvester)
14. Chapel of St Andrew
15. Chapel of St Wenceslas
16. Hasenburg Chapel
17. Thun Chapel
18. Chapel of the Holy Sepulchre
19. Chapel of St Ludmila
20. Main entrance and façade
21. Golden Gate
22. Great Tower with belfry

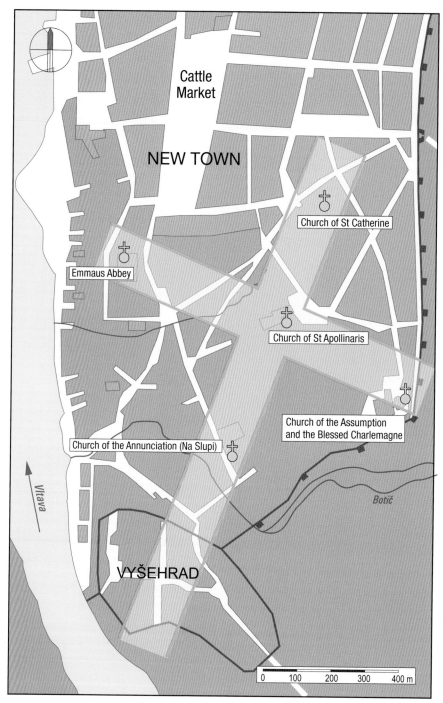

Map of the New Town of Prague with planned built-up areas, *c.*1378.

THE CAROLINE CROSS OF PRAGUE

The architectural idea of a mystical cross marked out by the placing of five New Town churches is probably connected with Charles's spiritual conception of the New Town. The east-west arm of the cross is formed by the Emmaus Abbey, St Apollinaris' Church and Karlov; the north-south arm is formed

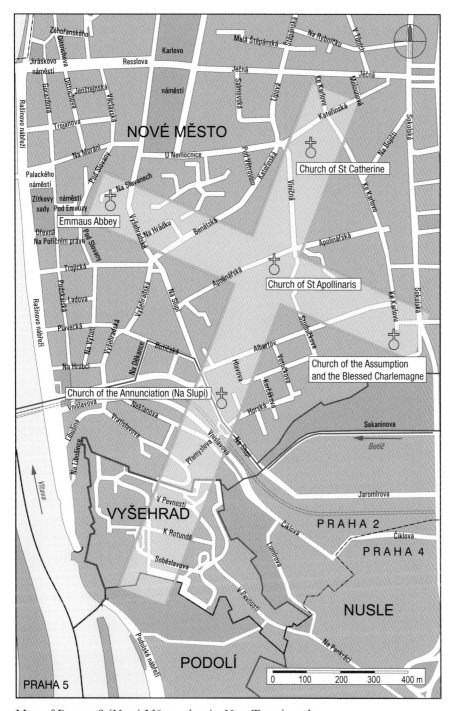

Map of Prague 2 (Nové Město, that is, New Town), today.

by St Catherine's, St Apollinaris' (the point of intersection), and the
Church of the Madonna of Humility (kostel Panny Marie Na Slupi);
in the extension it then touches Vyšehrad. The idea of a cross was meant
to secure a special blessing on Charles's city.

(193)

ACKNOWLEDGEMENTS

The Karolinum Press thanks the galleries, museums and owners and keepers of art collections, particularly the Prague Castle Administration (Správa Pražského hradu), for having generously provided illustrations for this publication and for granting permission to publish them.

LIST OF ILLUSTRATIONS

Cover: The gem-encrusted walls of St Wenceslas Chapel – detail.
Dust-jacket flap: St Vitus' Cathedral, looking east.
Pages 1–12:
Architectural details of the Cathedral, Správa Pražského hradu. Photo Jan Gloc, Prague.
The Carolinum – oriel. Photo Cyril Royt, Prague.
The Bohemian Crown, Správa Pražského hradu. Photo Jan Gloc, Prague.
Charles Bridge. Photo Cyril Royt, Prague.
Face of Charles IV – detail from the *Votive Panel Painting of John Očko of Vlašim*.

I. Documentary photographs

The Bohemian Crown, 1344–45, Kancelář prezidenta republiky, Správa Pražského hradu. Photo Jan Gloc, Prague, p. 15.

Bust of Matthew of Arras, triforium of St Vitus' Cathedral, 1380–82, Metropolitní kapitula u sv. Víta, Správa Pražského hradu. Photo Jan Gloc, Prague, p. 18.

Bust of Peter Parler, triforium of St Vitus' Cathedral, 1380–82, Metropolitní kapitula u sv. Víta, Správa Pražského hradu. Photo Jan Gloc, Prague, p. 19.

Bust of Benedict Krabice of Weitmühle – triforium of St Vitus' Cathedral, 1380–82, Metropolitní kapitula u sv. Víta, Správa Pražského hradu. Photo Jan Gloc, Prague, p. 22.

The Foundation Charter of Prague University, 7 April 1348, Charles University, Prague, Archive of Nakladatelství Karolinum. Photo Oto Palán, Prague, p. 25.

Seal impression of Prague University, mid-14th century, Charles University, Prague, archive of Nakladatelství Karolinum. Photo Oto Palán, Prague, p. 26.

Silver seal matrix of Prague University, mid-14th century, Charles University, Prague, archive of Nakladatelství Karolinum. Photo Oto Palán, Prague, p. 27.

The New Town of Prague – map, adapted by Jaroslav Synek, p. 30.

Chapel of Corpus Christi, model from Sadeler's veduta of Prague, 1606, archive of the author, p. 32.

The Lands of the Bohemian Crown in the reign of Charles IV, adapted by Jaroslav Synek, p. 34.

The Holy Roman Empire in the reign of Charles IV, adapted by Jaroslav Synek, p. 35.

The Golden Bull – the Emperor and Empress at a banquet, 1356, MS from 1400, ÖNB Vienna, after František Šmahel, *The Parisian Summit, 1377–78: Emperor Charles IV and King Charles V of France*. Prague: Karolinum, 2014 (p. 79), p. 37.

The Golden Bull – Seal impression. Charles IV as Emperor of the Holy Roman Emperor and King of Bohemia, 1356, ÖNB Vienna, after František Šmahel, *The Parisian Summit, 1377–78: Emperor Charles IV and King Charles V of France*. Prague: Karolinum, 2014 (p. 65), p. 37.

'Charles IV's Dream in Terenzo', *Vita Caroli*, 1356, MS from 1472, ÖNB Vienna, Cod. Ser. N. 2618, fol. 27v, 21 × 15 cm, after František Šmahel, *The Parisian Summit, 1377–78: Emperor Charles IV and King Charles V of France*. Prague: Karolinum, 2014 (p. 52), p. 38.

Bust of Ernest of Pardubice, triforium of St Vitus' Cathedral, Správa Pražského hradu. Photo Jan Gloc, Prague, p. 40.

Bust of John Očko of Vlašim, triforium of St Vitus' Cathedral, Správa Pražského hradu. Photo Jan Gloc, Prague, p. 41.

Bust of John of Jenstein, triforium of St Vitus' Cathedral, Správa Pražského hradu. Photo Jan Gloc, Prague, p. 41.

Votive Panel Painting of John Očko of Vlašim, before 1371, tempera on wood, 181 × 96 cm, Národní galerie v Praze, pp. 42–43.

Votive Panel Painting of John Očko of Vlašim – detail of Charles IV's face.

Liber viaticus of John of Neumarkt, c.1360, Národní muzeum, Prague, KNM XIII A 12, pp. 44–45.

Miniature with Bishop John of Neumarkt, *Liber viaticus of John of Neumarkt*.

Drollery, detail from the *Liber viaticus of John of Neumarkt*.

Noah's Arc, from the *Velislai biblia picta*, 1325–49, Prague, Národní knihovna ČR, NK XXIII.C. 124, 9, p. 47.

Breviary of Grand Master Leo, sv. Anežka Česká, 1356, Prague, Knihovna Rytířského řádu, Křižovníků s červenou hvězdou, deposited in the Národní knihovna ČR, XVIII.F.6, p. 48.

Miniature of Charles IV as King of the Romans and King of Bohemia, *Gelnhausen Codex*, late 14th, early 15th century, Státní okresní archiv Jihlava, oddělení Úřední knihy a rukopisy, inv. 17, f. 56r, p. 49.

Theodoric of Prague, *The Blessed Charlemagne*, before 1365, tempera on wood, 116 × 87.2 cm, Chapel of the Holy Cross, Karlstein, Národní památkový ústav středních Čech, on loan to the Národní galerie v Praze, p. 50.

Zbraslav Madonna, 1345–50, tempera and gilding on canvas-covered wood, 89 × 60 cm, Parish of St James the Great, Zbraslav, ŘKF u kostela sv. Jakuba Většího Praha–Zbraslav, on loan to the Národní galerie v Praze, p. 51.

Conrad Waldhauser, *Postilla studentium sanctae Pragensis universitatis*, Národní knihovna ČR, XX. A.14, 1r (4) 685, p. 52.

John Milíč of Kroměříž, *Sermones*, MS, Národní knihovna ČR, NK IX A 5, FS, p. 53.

Royal Entry into Paris, *Grandes chroniques de France*, 1375–80, after František Šmahel, *The Parisian Summit, 1377–78: Emperor Charles IV and King Charles V of France*. Prague: Karolinum, 2014 (p. 203), p. 55.

Banquet – Charles IV, the Holy Roman Emperor, and Charles V of France, watching a re-enactment of the taking of Jerusalem in the First Crusade, *Grandes chroniques de France*, 1375–80, after František Šmahel, *The Parisian Summit, 1377–78: Emperor Charles IV and King Charles V of France*. Prague: Karolinum, 2014 (p. 212), p. 56.

Master of the Luxembourg Genealogy, *Relic Scenes*, c.1357, wall painting, the Lady Chapel at Karlstein, after Jan Royt, *Středověké malířství v Čechách*, Prague: Karolinum, 2002 (p. 65), p. 58.

Frontispiece, p. 60: Prague Castle and Charles Bridge. Photo Oto Palán, Prague.

II. A Guide to Prague

1A–C/ St Vitus' Cathedral at Prague Castle, founded on 21 November 1344: whole and details of the buttresses, Metropolitní kapitula u sv. Víta, Správa Pražského hradu. Photo Jan Gloc, Prague.

1D–F/ Golden Gate of St Vitus' Cathedral, Prague Castle, 1367–71, Metropolitní kapitula u sv. Víta, Správa Pražského hradu. Photo Jan Gloc, Prague.

2/ Choir of St Vitus' Cathedral, looking east, Metropolitní kapitula u sv. Víta, Správa Pražského hradu. Photo Jan Gloc, Prague.

3A–F/ From the Treasury of St Vitus' Cathedral.

A–B/ Golden reliquary cross of the Kingdom of Bohemia, obverse & reverse, base from the 13th century, altered *c*.1357, Svatovítský poklad, Metropolitní kapitula u sv. Víta, Správa Pražského hradu. Photo Jan Gloc, Prague.

C/ Onyx chalice of Charles IV, 1350, Svatovítský poklad, Metropolitní kapitula u sv. Víta, Správa Pražského hradu. Photo Jan Gloc, Prague.

D–E/ Gothic reliquary of the Parler type, obverse & reverse, *c*.1400, Svatovítský poklad, Metropolitní kapitula u sv. Víta, Správa Pražského hradu. Photo Jan Gloc, Prague.

F/ *Vera Icon*, 1400–10, Svatovítský poklad, Metropolitní kapitula u sv. Víta, Správa Pražského hradu. Photo Jan Gloc, Prague.

4/ Royal burial place in St Vitus' Cathedral – tomb of Ottokar I Přemysl, by Peter Parler, 1377, Metropolitní kapitula u sv. Víta, Správa Pražského hradu. Photo Jan Gloc, Prague.

5/ Corbel with Adam and Eve, St Vitus' Cathedral, after 1356, Metropolitní kapitula u sv. Víta, Správa Pražského hradu. Photo Jan Gloc, Prague.

6A–H/ Inner triforium of St Vitus' Cathedral, 1375–80: (A) John of Luxembourg, (B) Elizabeth of Bohemia, (C) Charles IV, (D) Blanche of Valois, (E) Anne of Bavaria (Anne of the Palatinate), (F) Anne of Schweidnitz, (G) Elizabeth of Pomerania, (H) Wenceslas IV, Metropolitní kapitula u sv. Víta, Správa Pražského hradu. Photo Jan Gloc, Prague.

7/ A dog and a cat fighting, inner triforium of St Vitus' Cathedral, Prague Castle, 1375–80, Metropolitní kapitula u sv. Víta, Správa Pražského hradu. Photo Jan Gloc, Prague.

8/ St Wenceslas, outer triforium of St Vitus' Cathedral, Metropolitní kapitula u sv. Víta, Správa Pražského hradu. Photo Jan Gloc, Prague.

9A–H/ St Wenceslas Chapel, St Vitus' Cathedral, Metropolitní kapitula u sv. Víta, Správa Pražského hradu. Photo Jan Gloc, Prague.
(A) looking northwest, (B) tabernacle in the St Wenceslas Chapel, 1375; (C–D) the gem-encrusted walls, (E) the Flagellation of Christ from the Passion cycle, (G) corbel with St Peter, (H) corbel with Judas and the Devil.

10/ Statute of St Wenceslas, *c*.1373, Metropolitní kapitula u sv. Víta, Správa Pražského hradu. Photo Jan Gloc, Prague.

11/ *Baptism of St Odilia*, Vlašim Chapel, St Vitus' Cathedral, Metropolitní kapitula u sv. Víta, Správa Pražského hradu. Photo Jan Gloc, Prague.

12/ Saxon Chapel, St Vitus' Cathedral, *Adoration of the Magi*, Metropolitní kapitula u sv. Víta, Správa Pražského hradu. Photo Jan Gloc, Prague.

13/ Church of All Saints, Prague Castle, founded in 1341, Správa Pražského hradu. Photo Jan Gloc, Prague.

14/ Palace of Charles IV, Prague Castle, Správa Pražského hradu. Photo Jan Gloc, Prague.

15/ Bishop's Court, tower. Photo Cyril Royt, Prague.

16A–B/ The Church of Our Lady under the Chain, after 1314, whole and detail. Photo Cyril Royt.

17/ Hunger Wall, 1360–62. Photo Cyril Royt, Prague.

18/ Charles Bridge, founded in 1357. Photo Oto Palán, Prague.

19A–E/ Old Town Bridge Tower, from the 1370s–80s, whole and details. Photo Cyril Royt, Prague.

20A–B/ Town Hall, Old Town, tower from the 1360s, Madonna, 1356–57. Photo Cyril Royt, Prague.

21A–D/ Thein Church, 3rd quarter of the 14th century, whole, north portal and details. Photo Cyril Royt, Prague.

22A–F/ Stone Bell House, whole and details, wall paintings c.1340. Photo Cyril Royt, Prague.

23A–F/ Carolinum, chapel with oriel and its details (A–C), photo Cyril Royt, Prague; window seat, university treasury and archive) (D–F), 1375–1376, photo Oto Palán, Prague.

24/ Church of the Holy Spirit, 2nd quarter of the 14th century. Photo Cyril Royt, Prague.

25/ Church of St Castulus, founded c.1310. Photo Cyril Royt, Prague.

26A–B/ Church of St Giles, whole and detail, consecrated 1371. Photo Cyril Royt, Prague.

27A–F/ Church of St Anne, built in 1319–30, wall paintings from 1370s and 1380s, now the Prague Crossroads. Photo Cyril Royt, Prague.

28/ Church of St Martin in the Wall, rebuilt in 1350–58. Photo Cyril Royt, Prague.

29A–D/ Church of Our Lady of the Snow, founded 1347, whole and details. Photo Cyril Royt, Prague.

30/ New Town town hall, 1371–98, 1411, and 16th century. Photo Cyril Royt, Prague.

31A–K/ Emmaus Abbey, founded 1347, wall paintings 1358–62. Photo Cyril Royt, Prague.

32/ Steeples of the Church of St Apollinaris, founded in 1362, and the Church of St Catherine, founded in 1355. Photo Cyril Royt, Prague.

33A–D/ Church of St Apollinaris, whole, nave , wall paintings, c.1380. Photo Cyril Royt.

34/ Church of the Assumption and the Blessed Charlemagne, founded in 1350. Photo Cyril Royt, Prague.

35/ Church of the Annunciation (also the Church of Our Lady of Humility; kostel Panny Marie Pokorné, kostel Panny Marie na Slupi, or Panny Marie na Slupi na Trávníčku), founded in 1360. Photo Cyril Royt, Prague.

36/ Church of St Stephen, founded in 1348. Photo Cyril Royt, Prague.

37/ Church of Sts Henry and Cunigunde, founded in 1348. Photo Cyril Royt, Prague.

38/ The Church of St Wenceslas at Zderaz, rebuilt in a Gothic style, c.1350–79. Photo Cyril Royt, Prague.

39/ Vyšehrad with the Basilica of Sts Peter and Paul. Photo Cyril Royt, Prague.

40/ *Vyšehrad Madonna* (*Madonna of the Rain*), c.1360, tempera on a wood, 68.5 × 54 cm, Collegiate Church of Sts Peter and Paul, Prague, on loan to the Národní galerie v Praze.

JAN ROYT, PhDr, Ing., PhD (1955)

After graduating from agricultural college in Prague and then receiving a doctorate in art history at Charles University, Prague, Jan Royt worked from 1984 to 1990 as an editor of art-history publications at Odeon Publishers, Prague. After the Changes of 1990, he became a senior lecturer at the Institute of Art History, Charles University, and habilitated in 1997. He was made a professor of Charles University in 2004. Since 2006 he has been Director of the Institute of Art History at Charles University. He also teaches at the Catholic Faculty of Theology (Charles University), the Academy of Fine Arts, Prague, and Purkyně University, Ústí nad Labem, and is on the Academic Board both of Charles University, Prague, and of Masaryk University, Brno. In 2014, he was appointed Vice-Chancellor of Charles University for Projects and Publishing.

His research interests are in art history, ranging from the Early Christian period to the end of the Baroque, particularly medieval painting and Christian iconography. He has participated in a number of exhibitions, both Czech and international, including 'St John Nepomucene, 1393–1993', 'Theodoric of Prague', and 'Charles IV, Emperor by the Grace of God'. He is the author of several books and more than 200 academic articles published in the Czech Republic and abroad.

Awards
1994: The Josef Krása Prize, awarded by the Czech Association of Art Historians
2010: The Gold Medal of St Vitus', awarded by Dominik Duka, Archbishop of Prague and Primate of Bohemia.

Publications (a selection)
Obraz a kult v Čechách v 17. a 18. století (Karolinum, 1999, 2011)
Medieval Painting in Bohemia (Karolinum, 2003)
Mittelalterliche Malerei in Böhmen (Karolinum, 2003)
Slovník biblické ikonografie (Karolinum, 2007)
The Master of the Třeboň Altarpiece (Karolinum, 2014)

This series is devoted to the history of Prague, with a focus on the arts and intellectual life of the city. In a factual yet lively way it seeks to give an informed account of the thousand-year development of the city with its changes, both intellectual and material, and its legendary *genius loci*, thus contributing to general knowledge about Czech culture.

A typical volume in the series comprises a comprehensive account of the topic, accompanied by illustrations and 'walks through Prague', by means of photographs of the preserved historical architecture and other works of art together with commentary. The publication includes a list of important historical figures, an index with corresponding maps of the location of the art and architecture, and a bibliography.

The contributors to this series are respected Prague art historians, photographers, and translators.